Contributions to Economics

The series *Contributions to Economics* provides an outlet for innovative research in all areas of economics. Books published in the series are primarily monographs and multiple author works that present new research results on a clearly defined topic, but contributed volumes and conference proceedings are also considered. All books are published in print and ebook and disseminated and promoted globally. The series and the volumes published in it are indexed by Scopus and ISI (selected volumes).

Cristina Peicuti

The European Economy in 100 Quotes

A Guide to Crucial Economic Ideas

Springer

Cristina Peicuti
ESCP Business School
Paris, France

ISSN 1431-1933 ISSN 2197-7178 (electronic)
Contributions to Economics
ISBN 978-3-031-68818-8 ISBN 978-3-031-68819-5 (eBook)
https://doi.org/10.1007/978-3-031-68819-5

This Springer imprint is published by the registered company Springer Nature Switzerland AG
The registered company address is: Gewerbestrasse 11, 6330 Cham, Switzerland

Fit homo, non nascitur

"Man is not born, but made man"

Erasmus [1466–1535]

To my friends of Haus 13,

Strümpelstrasse 6, Düsseldorf, Germany:

Erasmus exchanges

Jennifer, Stefanie (Antwerp), Guy (Ostend), Roberta (Florence), Sarah (Wickford), Ray, Elaine (Dublin), Arnaud, Maëlle (Lorient), Celeste (Apricena), Katinka (Budapest), Milena (Prague), Sabrina (Naples), Edna (Celje), Mariya (Perm), Irene (A Coruña), Marta, Michal, Ewelina, Tomasz, Agnieszka (Gdansk), Elias (Alicante), Graham (Wales), Marko (Maribor), Natasha (Slovenia), Juan Carlos (Jaén), Miguel (Mérida), Cristina (Pamplona), and Désirée (Ourense)

Other exchange programmes

Lina, Guillermo, Nicolas (Medellin), David (Philadelphia), Vadim (Minsk), and Stanislav (Saint-Petersburg)

Note from the Author

Except for Greek and Roman authors, quotes are presented under the country of birth of the authors based on current national boundaries.

There is no wealth or strength except in men.

—Jean Bodin [1529–1596], *Les six livres de la République*

We do not inherit the earth from our parents, we borrow it from our children.

—Antoine de Saint-Exupéry [1900–1944], *Terre des hommes*

Acknowledgement

Translated with the support of the chair of BPCE Group at the ESCP Business School on Mutual and Cooperative Banking for the Benefit of the Economy.

Contents

Introduction

Europe is characterised by two things: an economy and a civilisation that have been intertwined for thousands of years.

Hippocrates [460–370 BC], traditionally regarded as the father of Medicine, was one of the first to describe the *Europaios*, whom he said were defined by physical, moral and political characteristics derived from the topography and climate. Hippocrates' theory has had an extraordinary influence over the centuries, changing the worldview of an entire continent whose inhabitants have come to define themselves as *Europaios*.

The word 'economy' can be traced to the Ancient Greek *oikonomia,* which means 'organisation'.[1]

This Greek word is in turn composed of two words: *oikos*, which is usually translated as 'household' (and which the Greek philosopher opposes to *polis*, referring to the 'city') and *nemein*, which is best translated as 'management and dispensation'. In Ancient Greece, the word 'economy' referred to the household not just in the sense of a family consumption unit, but more in the sense of an estate producing the wealth from which the owner and his family lived.[2]

With the emergence of the Nation-State at the end of the Middle Ages, the economy is no longer confined to household management but is a matter for the city or the state. From this came the term 'economic policy', from the Greek *oikonomia* and *polis*. In France, the term was coined by one of the country's first

---

[1] https://www.larousse.fr/dictionnaires/francais/%C3%A9conomie/27630

[2] Leshem, Dotan (2016), *Retrospectives: What Did the Ancient Greeks Mean by Oikonomia?*, Journal of Economic Perspectives, vol. 30, no. 1.

C. Peicuti, *The European Economy in 100 Quotes*, Contributions to Economics,
https://doi.org/10.1007/978-3-031-68819-5_1

economists, Antoine de Montchrestien [1574–1621]), who published a *Traicte de l'oeconomie politiqve dédié av Roy et à la Reyne Mère du Roy* in 1615.

As French writer Ernest Renan [1823–1892] explained: "What constitutes a nation is not speaking the same language, or belonging to a common ethnographic group, but being a body of people having done great things together and wishing to do more."[3] From an economic and cultural standpoint, Europe would fit this definition.

Back in 1882, Ernest Renan's view was that: "Nations are not eternal. They have a beginning and they will have an end. And they will probably be replaced by a European confederation."[4]

The two world wars resulted in the rise of the United States and the Soviet Union, both invited by the belligerent European nations to wade into the conflict. The Soviet Union took advantage of the Second World War to conquer half of Europe and impose communism and the command economy. The other half of Europe came under the influence of the United States and retained a market economy. But great statesmen like De Gaulle sought to limit American influence by checking its inroads.

In 1987, 2 years before the fall of the Berlin Wall, French philosopher and sociologist Edgar Morin [1921–] lamented this political evolution: "Europe has shrunk. It is now just a fragment of the West, whereas just four centuries ago the West was just a fragment of Europe."[5]

In the 1950s, the Romanian philosopher Emil Cioran [1911–1995], who fled communism and sought refuge in France, would lament: "How can we count on the awakening, on the anger of Europe? Its fate and even its revolts are settled elsewhere."[6]

Stephan Zweig [1881–1942], in his autobiography, *The World of Yesterday: Memoirs of a European*, was the first to write with nostalgia about Europe before the First World War.[7] Four decades later, 2 years before the fall of the Berlin Wall, in his essay *The Art of the Novel,* Czech writer Milan Kundera, who like Emil Cioran

[3]Renan, Ernest (1882), *Qu'est-ce qu'une nation?*, réédition Paris, Imprimerie nationale, 1996.

[4]Ibid.

[5]Morin, Edgar (1987), *Concept of Europe*, Holmes & Meier Publishers.

[6]Cioran, Emil (1956), *La tentation d'exister*, Paris, Gallimard.

[7]Zweig, Stefan (1943), *The World of Yesterday: Memoirs of a European*, New York, The Viking Press.

went into exile in France, defined a "European [as] one who is nostalgic for Europe."[8]

Now, having been reunified, and as the world's second-largest power, the European Union finds itself torn economically between the United States and China, with a war on its doorstep. It was its acceptance into the World Trade Organisation in 2001 without any real obligation to abide by the rules imposed on other members that enabled China to develop, to the point where it is attempting to wrestle global economic and political leadership from the United States, and which had been Europe's until the Second World War.

Such is the world... unless young Europeans have other ideas and want Europe to reclaim its global leadership. When you are second, you are just one step off the top of the podium. In the grand scheme of things, Georg Hegel [1770–1831] saw Europe at the end of History, in his words "World history travels from east to west; for Europe is the absolute end of History, just as Asia is the beginning."[9]

In geographical terms, this annotated anthology covers the 27 countries of the European Union, the United Kingdom and Norway. Chronologically, the book extends from Greek antiquity to the present day. Through insights and quotes from leading European thinkers, economists, sociologists, novelists, playwrights, politicians and all the European Nobel laureates in economic sciences, it serves as a crucial initial guide to European economic ideas, inviting the reader to explore more extensively the quoted sources.

Europe is our common good. This anthology invites us to think of Europe in socio-economic terms, and thus discover that these terms vary little from one European country to another or over two and a half thousand years. The painful interlude of 45 years of communism imposed by Soviet Union on half of Europe after the Second World War was a contrived interruption in our economic and cultural history. It ended with the fall of the Berlin Wall in 1989. The quotes in the book confirm that, despite what Soviet Union tried to impose as its *Weltanschauung*, there has indeed been just the one Europe over the centuries, not a so-called Eastern Europe and so-called Western Europe. I dedicate this book to my Erasmus year in Düsseldorf where, 13 years after the fall of the Wall, in Haus 13, I celebrated European sisterhood and brotherhood. No tensions or arguments overshadowed this European communal living. The same year saw the release of the French film *Une auberge espagnole*, which captured the atmosphere of an Erasmus flat-share but did not reflect the fall of the Wall. Our hall of residence on

---

[8] https://www.lemonde.fr/en/opinion/article/2023/07/17/milan-kundera-outlined-a-certain-idea-of-europe_6056272_23.html

[9] Hegel, Georg Wilhelm Friedrich (1832), *Lectures on the Philosophy of World History, Introduction, Reason in History.*

Strümpelstrasse was home to Europeans from one half of Europe finally reunited with its other half. The reunification was as natural as the separation had been artificial.

This book was originally intended for students at the École de Commerce Supérieure de Paris (ESCP Business School), founded in 1819, a truly European seat of learning with campuses in London, Paris, Berlin, Turin, Madrid and Warsaw. The book was written more generally for the public at large, because the market economy and Europe represent our living environment, the constant of our existence for thousands of years.

The topics were chosen according to this constant, after researching European digital libraries and exchanging with their documentalists to identify the most recurring, most discussed economic topics in each country. The book attempts to combine the insider's perspective, provided by documentalists in each country, with that of the outsider, the European economic researcher that I am, in order to give a true picture of national economic concerns. Even if the specific concerns of each European country vary, the discourse is the same: it is not that of the triumph of commodity fetishism and the reign of the Golden Calf; it is about the longing for the freedom of enterprise, for a market economy based on competition, for the fight against corruption, for a fair distribution of wealth, for an economy at the service of mankind and therefore of the planet. For this reason, the book begins with these two quotes:

> There is no wealth or strength except in men.
> Jean Bodin [1529–1596], *Les six livres de la République*

> We do not inherit the earth from our parents, we borrow it from our children.
> Antoine de Saint-Exupéry [1900–1944], *Terre des hommes*

As Joyce would put it: "Moses begat Noah and Noah begat Eunuch and Eunuch begat O'Halloran and O'Halloran begat Guggenheim and Guggenheim begat Agendath and Agendath begat Netaim and Netaim begat Le Hirsch and Le Hirsch begat Jesurum and Jesurum begat MacKay and MacKay begat Ostrolopsky and Ostrolopsky begat Smerdoz and Smerdoz begat Weiss and Weiss begat Schwarz and Schwarz begat Adrianopoli and Adrianopoli begat Aranjuez and Aranjuez begat Lewy Lawson and Lewy Lawson begat Ichabudonosor and Ichabudonosor begat O'Donnell Magnus and O'Donnell Magnus begat Christbaum and Christbaum begat ben Maimun and ben Maimun begat Dusty Rhodes and Dusty Rhodes begat Benamor and Benamor begat Jones-Smith and Jones-Smith begat Savorgnanovich and Savorgnanovich begat Jasperstone and Jasperstone begat Vingtetunieme and Vingtetunieme begat Szombathely and Szombathely begat Virag and Virag begat Bloom et vocabitur nomen eius Emmanuel."[10]

---

[10]Source: Joyce, James, Ulysses, Planet pdf, retrieved from, https://web.itu.edu.tr/inceogl4/modernism/Ulysses.pdf

Greece

Money

In several languages, Ancient Greek but also French, the term silver (*árgyros* in Ancient Greek, argent in French) refers to silver pieces or coins as well as the precious metal. Alexander the Great's father, when he consulted the Oracle in Delphi, was told: "With silver spears you may conquer the world". Having seized the silver mines in neighbouring Thracian and Illyrian kingdoms, he used the silver extracted from these mines to bribe his way to early victories.

Alcaeus of Mytilene [630–580 BC], denouncing the power of money, wrote:

> In Sparta once Aristodemus,
> So the story ran,
> A maxim full of wisdom uttered:
> "Money makes the man."
> For valour leaves the wretch that's poor,
> And honour shuns the pauper's door.[1]

In Antigone, the Greek dramatist Sophocles [495–406 BC] wrote:

> Money!
> Money's the curse of man, none greater.
> That's what wrecks cities, banishes men from homes,
> Tempts and deludes the most well-meaning soul,
> Pointing out the way to infamy and shame.

[1] Easby-Smith, James S (1901), *The Songs of Alcaeus, memoir and text*, with literal translations and notes by James S Easby-Smith, W H Lowdermilk: Washington, p. 85. http://archive.org/stream/songsofalcaeusme00alcauoft#page/84/mode/2up

C. Peicuti, *The European Economy in 100 Quotes*, Contributions to Economics,
https://doi.org/10.1007/978-3-031-68819-5_2

And he lamented that "There's nothing in the world so demoralising as money".

Menander [343–292 BC], a Greek dramatist and the best-known representative of Athenian New Comedy, wrote that: "It is gold that holds power over men"; and that: "Silver opens everything, even bronze doors". This last maxim inspired a French proverb *L'argent ouvre tout, même les portes de bronze* ("A silver hammer can break an iron door"), the German version referring to a golden hammer. Still alluding to money's power for opening all doors, in his *L'École des femmes*,[2] French playwright Molière wrote: "Money is the master key to all great plans".[3]

Timing

In business, recognising the right moment and seizing it is essential for success. In finance, it is about finding a "window of opportunity" to float a company, launch a product, or propose a project; in other words, timing is of the essence.

The Greek saying *Kaïron gnothi* ("Know thine opportunity") was attributed to Pittacus of Mytilene [640–570 BC], one of the Seven Sages of Greece.

A Greek proverb states that: "The year, not the land, determines the harvest".

In *Gorgias*, a Socratic dialogue written by Plato [428–348 BC], referring to people having missed something that would have been to their benefit, Callicles, one of the sophists said: "The wise man, as the proverb says, is late for a fray, but not for a feast".[4]

Urging one to seize the moment when it came without delay, the Greek theologian Gregory of Nazianzus [329–390] wrote: "While the iron is hot, let it be tempered by the cold water, lest anything should happen in the interval, and put an end to your desire".[5]

---

[2] *School for Wives*

[3] Molière (2001), *The School for Wives*, Blackmask Online, http://www.searchengine.org.uk/ebooks/85/18.pdf

[4] https://freeclassicebooks.com/Plato/Gorgias.pdf

[5] https://www.newadvent.org/fathers/310240.htm

Opportunity

Greek sophist Anaxarchus [380–320 BC] held that the ability to seize the "opportune moment" (*kairos*) was the boundary marker of wisdom.

Greek poet Posidippus [310–240 BC] wrote an epigram interpreting the details of a statue by Lysippus named *Kairos* (Ancient Greek for opportune moment): "The occasion that governs everything".

Michel Apostolius [1420–1478], who taught for a short time at the Monastery of St. John of Petra in Constantinople, published a collection of Greek proverbs, one stating that: "Occasion makes for bold action".

The ancient Greeks also said that: "Opportunity is the accomplice of many things".

Business Start-Up

Greek proverbs warn that: "Starting anything is long and steep and rough at first", and that "Well begun is half done".

Greek historian Herodotus [480–425 BC] also warned that: "Every end does not appear together with its beginning".

Success

To succeed is an undertaking, Greek philosopher Aristotle [384–322 BC] warning that one cannot be sparing in one's efforts: "Fire a thousand arrows and you will end up catching something".

Greek poet and writer Nicarchus [first century AD] urged perseverance in undertaking any project, writing in one of his epigrams: "Leave no stone unturned".

Luxury

Pepper has been around for a long time, as attested by the X-ray study of the mummy of Ramses II [1304–1213 BC], which revealed that black peppercorns were placed in the nasal cavity. For centuries, pepper was a great luxury that only the immensely rich could afford. To denounce the useless luxuries of the rich, Michael Apostolius wrote: "He who has pepper in abundance also garnishes his salad with it", a maxim still uttered today by the natives of Corsica.

Savings

Between the fifteenth and nineteenth centuries, there were frequent remarks about saving candle-ends, which has survived to this day in the French language in the expression "*faire des économies de bouts de chandelles*". In Works and Days by the Ancient Greek poet Hesiod [750–650 BC], the idea is the same but with reference to the amphora of wine, his advice being: "Take your fill when the cask is first opened and when it is nearly spent, but midways be sparing: it is poor saving when you come to the lees".[6]

Wealth

Menander considered that: "No just person ever became quickly rich".

According to Michel Apostolius, people who are always moving, with no roots in one place or another, would not accumulate wealth, for he wrote: "A rolling stone gathers no moss". Lucius Seneca [4 BC–65 AD] would recall a proverb saying much the same: "A plant too often moved weakens".

According to Menander: "Riches are man's greatest shield".

In *De Constantia Sapientis*, a moral essay written by Seneca, the author recounts an exchange between Stilpon [360–280 BC] and Demetrius I of Macedon, also called Poliorcetes, after the latter had conquered and pillaged Megara, Stilpon's home town, in which this philosopher of great reputation when asked whether the soldiers have taken anything from him, replied: "All that's mine I carry with me".

Poverty

For Menander: "The discourses of the poor are in vain".

[6]https://www.gutenberg.org/cache/epub/348/pg348-images.html

Menander considered that there is "No burden so intolerable as poverty".[7]

A Greek proverb states: "No poor can afford prime quality meat", which remains true to this day.

In Plato's *Symposium*, in a dialogue between Socrates and Diotima, the high priestess from Mantinea recalls how Penia (the personification of poverty) because of her straitened circumstances, plotted to have a child with Poros (the personification of abundance, but also resourcefulness or expediency), accordingly she lay down at his side and conceived Eros (the personification of love), forever in need because of his mother, forever pursuing because of his father. About Eros, Diotima explained that: "Love is [...] alive and flourishing at one moment when he is in plenty, and dead at another moment", which inspired this proverb: "When poverty comes in at the door, love flies out at the window".

Athenian historian and general Thucydides [460–395 BC] considered that: "As for poverty, no one need to be ashamed to admit it: the real shame is in not taking practical measures to escape from it".

Fortune

In economic as well as human affairs, "Men's fortunes are on a wheel, which in its turning suffers not the same man to prosper forever", which Greek historian Herodotus attributed to Croesus. Greek philosopher Plutarch, in his *Consolatio ad Apollonium*, describing changes in fortunes, wrote: "The wheel goes round, and of the rim now one and now another part is at the top",[8] which he attributed to an unknown Greek author.

Cleobulus, one of the Seven Sages of Greece, proffered the following advice: "Do not be arrogant in prosperity; if you fall into poverty, do not humble yourself".

The ancient Greeks recorded how nets would "catch fish while men slept", which came to describe a man lucky in business. For Sophocles: "The dice of Zeus always fall luckily".

[7] https://www.exclassics.com/anatomy/anat102.htm

[8] https://penelope.uchicago.edu/Thayer/E/Roman/Texts/Plutarch/Moralia/Consolatio_ad_Apollonium*.html#note13

Governance

Plato held that: "The measure of a man is what he does with power".

The Greek historian and geographer Strabo [60–20 BC] recommended that one should "Take the bull by the horns".

Greek proverbs advise not persevering in the errors of one's way: "It is disgraceful to stumble against the same stone twice"; also: "To blunder twice is not allowed in war".

The Athenian historian and general Thucydides [460–400 BC] recommended always impressing one's adversaries to keep them at bay. This implied that: "If you want peace, prepare for war". The lyric poet Pindar [519–428 BC] warned that: "War is dear to those who do not know of it. To those who have tried it, they shake in front of his coming".[9]

In *The Life of Solon*, Plutarch warned that: "In great affairs it is difficult to please all".[10]

In *De liberis educandis*, Plutarch advised the master not to rest on the disposition of hired persons, for even those persons will devote more attention if they know they must from time to time render account, citing a groom who had remarked that "nothing makes the horse so fat as the king's eye", adding that the master should himself take cognizance of "their instruction by means of their own eyes or their own ears".[11] His contemporary, Juvenal, in *The Satires*, asked: "But who is to guard the guardians?"[12]

The famous philosopher Diogenes [413–324 BC] warned against having too many decision-makers deal with one issue: "Caria's ruin was its many generals".

Teamwork is important, the Ancient Greeks considered that: "One is nobody". This later would prompt Homer [eighth century BC] to write in the Iliad: "For union is strength, and weakness comes of division".[13] It also inspired the French proverb: "*Homme seul est viande à loups*", or if you prefer "A lone man is meat for the wolf".

---

[9] Kyriazoglou, John (2015), *An Anthology of Short Stories and Sayings of Ancient Greece*

[10] https://penelope.uchicago.edu/Thayer/E/Roman/Texts/Plutarch/Lives/Solon*.html

[11] https://penelope.uchicago.edu/Thayer/E/Roman/Texts/Plutarch/Moralia/De_liberis_educandis*.html

[12] Juvenal 2011, *The Satires*, translated by A. S. Kline, https://www.poetryintranslation.com/PITBR/Latin/Juvenalhome.php

[13] https://www.gutenberg.org/files/43993/43993-h/43993-h.htm

Hesiod warned against accepting gifts: "Gifts blind the gods, gifts blind noble kings".

The playwright Aristophanes [445–c.385 BC) urges us to face difficulties head-on and to accept the consequences of our decisions and actions: "Since you allowed yourself to drink the wine, you must also empty the lees".

An entrepreneur cannot do otherwise.

Human Resources

As explained by the writer of fables Aesop [620–564 BC]: "The wicked who prosper gather others about themselves".

The Ancient Greeks warned that: "Acquitting the guilty was to condemn the innocent".

The Chief Executive Officer and senior managers must behave in an exemplary manner and make the right decisions if they want their subordinates to do the same.

Michel Apostolius made the point that "A fish begins to stink from the head", which found its way into the French language as: "*Quand un poisson commence à pourrir c'est toujours par la tête*"; and in English as: "The fish always stinks from the head downwards".[14]

For Plato: "Masters and slaves can never be friends".[15] Seneca argued that few people are born slaves, most becoming slaves of their own volition.

Ancient Greek writers emphasised the fact that the same people, depending on the circumstances, can behave in diametrically opposed ways, pointing out that it is "The same sun which melts wax hardens clay".

Solon [630–560 BC] stated: "One who inspires fear in many has much to be fearful about".

---

[14] Oxford Dictionary of Proverbs (6 ed.) (2015), edited by Jennifer Speake, Oxford University Press

[15] https://core.ac.uk/download/pdf/49282371.pdf

Reputation

A Greek maxim states: "The infamy of just one citizen shames the city".

In *Pericles' Funeral Oration*, Thucydides writes: "For the whole earth is the tomb of famous men; not only are they commemorated by columns and inscriptions in their own country, but in foreign lands there dwells also an unwritten memorial of them, graven not on stone but in the hearts of men".[16]

Risk-Taking

Greek poet Antiphanes [408–334 BC] urges us to think before taking risks: "Better poor on dry land than rich at sea".

Greek comic author Dinolochus [end of fifth century BC] urges us to carefully assess the risks before taking them: "He who spits on an ants' nest has swollen lips".

Profession

An ancient Greek proverb states: "The man without a profession is everyone's slave".

Corruption

In the *Republic*, Plato considers that the most virtuous of men, if he degenerates, can become the worst of them: "Nothing worse than the corruption of the best".

Confidentiality

Michael Apostolius warns those who talk too much: "The foolish chick readily shows where it nests".

---

[16] http://hrlibrary.umn.edu/education/thucydides.html

Persuasion

The art of persuasion is essential to doing business. To this end, Greek philosopher Antisthenes [440–362 BC] explained: "We must not contradict, but instruct him that contradicts us; for a madman is not cured by another running mad also".

Communication

Diogenes proffered the following advice: "Do not despise the orator who makes himself understood by the vulgar".

Taking Up a Business

In Book I of *Physics*, Aristotle makes the point: "A man investigating principles cannot argue with one who denies their existence".[17]

Applied to business, this cautions against doing business with someone who does not play by the rules.

Undertaking

In the *Republic*, Plato teaches us that: "The most beautiful undertakings are arduous".

Truth

In business, knowing the truth is vital.

In the *Nicomachean Ethics*, Aristotle explained that while both the truth and one's friends are loved: "It is a sacred thing to give the highest honour to the truth".

Truth must take precedence over everything, even friendship, for as the proverb said: "Plato is my friend, but truth is a better friend".

---

[17] https://people.bu.edu/wwildman/WeirdWildWeb/courses/wphil/readings/wphil_rdg07_physics_entire.htm

Italy

Ecology

In *De Finibus*, Roman statesman Marcus Tullius Cicero [106–43 BC] invited the reader to follow nature's example: *Parvo esset natura contenta* ("Nature is content with little").

One might add that nature does not produce waste and that mankind should do the same.

For the green revolution to succeed, the nature of man's needs must change, for as pointed out by Seneca [4 BC–65 AD]: *Is minimo eget mortalis qui minimum cupit* ("That man has the fewest wants, who is the least anxious for wealth"[1]).

Confidentiality

In *Phaedra*, Seneca's advice was: *Alium silere quod voles, primus sile* ("To make another person hold his tongue, be you first silent"[2]).

Request

In *Phaedra*, Seneca wrote: *Qui timide rogat, docet negare* ("He who asks timidly invites a refusal").

[1] https://quod.lib.umich.edu/m/moa/AJD1448.0001.001?rgn=main;view=fulltext

[2] Ibid.

C. Peicuti, *The European Economy in 100 Quotes*, Contributions to Economics,
https://doi.org/10.1007/978-3-031-68819-5_3

In *The Saturnalia*, Macrobius [370–430] wrote: *Potestas... et si supplicet cogit* ("From a man of power, even an invitation is in effect compulsion").

Corruption

In the *Epistles* published in 20 BC, Horace [65–8 BC] bemoaned Romans for adopting the motto: *Virtus post nummos ("Virtue after riches").*

In the *Odes*, Horace wrote that Virgil [70–19 BC] is *animae dimidium meae* ("the half of my soul"). In Virgil's *Aeneid*, witnessing the murder of Priam's youngest son, Polydorus, Aeneas lets out: *Quid non mortalia pectora cogis, auri sacra fames?* ("Accursed thirst of gold! To what dost not thou compel the human breast?").

Marcus Porcius Cato [234–149 BC] came to the conclusion that: *Fures privatorum in nervo atque in compedibus aetatem agunt, fures publici in auro atque in purpura* ("Those who practice private theft spend their lives in chains and fetters, public thieves in gold and purple").

Seneca concurred with this, writing: *Sacrilegia minuta puniuntur, magna in triumphis feruntur* ("Minor temple-robberies are punished; major ones are carried in triumphal processions").

This ancient wisdom has survived in several Italian expressions: "Commits a minor offence and you will end up in the galley, commits a major theft and you will make a career of it" and "Small thieves go to jail, big ones ride in carriages".

Gold has the last word: *Auro loquente omnis oratio inanis est* ("When gold speaks, the world falls silent").

In his *Epigrammata*, Marcus Valerius Martialis [40–104] said that many people offer gifts to obtain something more valuable in return: *Munera... misit in hamo* ("He sent the great gifts... but... on a hook").

A medieval text states that: "The Roman Curia does not look after sheep without wool: it listens to those who have their hands full, and closes the door on those who have empty hands".

Savings

As explained by the poet Puplilius Syrus [85–43 BC]: *Nullus est tam tutus quaestus quam quod habeas parcere* ("The surest income is the one you save").

Franco Modigliani [1918–2003], who was born in Rome, was awarded the 1985 Nobel Prize in Economics "for his pioneering analyses of saving and of financial markets". His acceptance speech was entitled *Life Cycle, Individual Thrift and the Wealth of Nations*.[3]

The life cycle hypothesis developed by Modigliani as early as 1954 contends that individuals plan their spending over their lifetimes, not just according to their current income as advanced by Keynes, but also according to their expected future income over the rest of their lifetime and their net wealth. Net wealth has an impact on consumption and evolves depending on the age of the individual: the young borrow and repay their debt, and when they move into middle age they start to accumulate wealth for their retirement: "Now the life cycle of family size, at least in the U.S., has a very humped shape rather similar to that of income, though with a somewhat earlier peak. As a result, one might expect, and generally finds a fairly constant rate of saving in the central age group, but lower saving or even dissaving in the very young or old".[4]

Therefore, according to Modigliani, the saving rate depends more on the age of the economic agent than the level of income or interest rate levels. This implies that it is the age structure of the population that determines the dynamism of consumption and saving rate. Modigliani considers that pay-as-you-go pension plans lead to lower savings.

In the 1986 edition of the *Revue française d'économie*, Franco Modigliani considered the correlation between the saving rate and growth rate, concluding that: "Between countries with identical individual behaviour the aggregate saving rate will be higher the higher the long run growth rate of the economy. It will be zero for zero growth".

Public Debt

As early as 1961, Franco Modigliani showed that if new spending by the State is financed by public debt rather than new taxes, it may be advantageous for those present at the time, but places a gross burden on those living beyond that time, and is in reality a net burden for society: had not the State taxed savings to meet this new spending, these savings would have financed investment.

A deficit concerns 1 year, whereas a debt is a stock or an accumulation of debts over several years. According to Modigliani: "The immediate effect of the deficit is

[3] https://www.nobelprize.org/uploads/2018/06/modigliani-lecture.pdf
[4] Ibid.

to make you feel good, like when you go on a trip and pay later. You feel good, and then you get a hangover. The deficit makes you feel good - until you pay later".

Economic Policy

Modigliani drew attention to the difference between the economy and economic policy, which must not be confused: "Economists agree about economics - and that's a science - and they disagree about economic policy because that's a value judgment... I've had profound disagreements on policy with the famous Milton Friedman. But, on economics, we agree".

Romano Prodi [1939–], who served as Italy's Prime Minister from 1996 to 1998 and from 2006 to 2008, and as the President of the European Commission from 1999 to 2004, declared in 2002: "Experience teaches us that misguided policies are generally pursued during the good times. It is an expansionary policy at the cycle peak that then deprives us of any leeway precisely when it is really needed".

Value

Franco Modigliani's contribution was not limited to macroeconomics but also spanned microeconomics. He can be considered the father of financial economy.

Whilst a professor at Carnegie Mellon's graduate school, Merton H. Miller [1923–2000] met Franco Modigliani, and the two turned their attention to corporate finance. In 1958, they published two theorems. The first, known as the Modigliani-Miller theorem, states that neither the volume nor the structure of debt affects the value of a company, provided that the financial markets function perfectly. The second, known as the dividend irrelevance theorem, states that a company's dividend policy does not affect its value in a perfect market. These theorems are based on the assumption that company directors seek to maximise the value of the company for shareholders. They do not maximise the rate of profit, but the market value of the company.

Several Latin maxims explain that the value of a good does not correspond to its purchase price but to *quanti emptorem invenerit* ("The price at which a buyer can be found"); and: *Res tantum valet quantum vendi potest* ("A good has no value to the extent it cannot be sold").

Work

Franco Modigliani's view was that: "A situation where people can grow old without having a job that rewards them individually while adding to the collective well-being is morally unacceptable".

Poverty

In his *Epigrammata*, Marcus Valerius Martialis wrote: *Semper pauper eris, si pauper es, [. . .] Dantur opes nullis nunc, nisi divitibus* ("You will always be poor [. . .] if you are already poor; nowadays wealth comes to no one but the rich"), which led to a French proverb that says: "All water into the river goes". This appears at odds with the trickle-down theory, which contends that if the rich get tax breaks, they will invest the extra money in the economy, the benefits of which would trickle down and enrich the working classes.

As explained by the poet Juvenal [55–128]: *Paupertatem summis ingeniis obesse, ne provehantur* ("It is not easy for men to rise whose qualities are thwarted by poverty".).

In *Fasti*, Ovid [43–18 BC] draws attention to the fact that: *Pauper ubique iacet* ("Everywhere poor are hidden"[5]).

In *De Providentia*, Seneca explained that: *Ignis aurum probat, miseria fortes viros* ("Fire is the test of gold; adversity, of strong men").

Wealth

In *Apologia*, Apuleius [125–170] wrote: *Neque laus in copia, neque culpa in penuria constitit* ("It is no credit to be rich and no disgrace to be poor").

Horace stated: *Crescentem sequitur cura pecuniam* ("Worry grows with the accumulation of wealth").

[5] Ovid, Fasti, Translated by A. S. Kline 2004.

Opportunity

It is from Virgil's Aeneid that comes the saying: *Audaces fortuna juvat* ("Fortune favours the bold").

In one of his distich, about the difficulty of seizing an opportunity, Cato explained that: *Fronte capillata est, post est Occasio calva* ("Time hath a Lock before, but's bald behind").

Risk

When facing an economic crisis, as any danger, some risk-taking is inevitable to prevail, as stressed by the poet Publilius Syrus [85–43 BC], brought as a slave to Rome and then freed by his master on account of his literary talent. One of his apophthegms reads: *Nunquam periculum sine periculo vincetur* ("Danger is never overcome without danger").

Plautus [254–184 BC] invites us to follow the example of the mouse: *Mus non uni fidit antro* ("A mouse does not rely on just one hole").

Entrepreneurship

One line in the *Metamorphoses* by Ovid captures the vision of entrepreneurs the likes of Gaston Gallimard, the eponymous founder of the illustrious French publishing house, or Jean-Luc Lagardère, who was at the origin of Airbus: *Sors tua mortalis non est mortale quod optas* ("Thy lot is mortal, and thou wishest what no mortal may").

To succeed, like Hercules, you must persevere: *Per aspera* ad astra ("Through adversities to the stars").

Leisure Industry

What would Roman philosopher Seneca have had to say about the leisure society, about the time spent on social networks or playing video games? In his *Letters from a Stoic*, he wrote: *Otium sine litteris mors est et hominis vivi sepultura* ("Leisure without literature is death or rather the burial of a living man").

Taxation

Two aphorisms by the Emperor Vespasian [9–79], quoted by the historian Suetonius [70–140 AD], have stood the test of time.

The best known: *Pecunia non olet* ("Money does not smell").

In ancient Rome, urine was valued for its ammonia content. To recoup spending on the construction of public urinals and fill the public coffers, Emperor Vespasian ordered the urine to be collected from the urinals and sold for use as a detergent, notably in tanning and wool production. This caused much discontent and was ridiculed. When Vespasian's son Titus alerted his father to this, his father held up a coin under his nose and asked him if he felt offended by its smell. When Titus said "No", the emperor replied: *Pecunia non olet.* The protests died down and the urinal became a symbol of civilisation, spreading throughout Europe, with Vespasian's name still attached to public urinals in Italy (*vespasiano*) and France (*vespasienne*).

In his *Satires*, Juvenal [55–128] adapted the famous formula to: *Lucri bonus ex re qualibet* ("The odour of gain is sweet, no matter its source").

The second aphorism is an exhortation from Vespasian to his prefects not to burden the people with taxes, because too many taxes kill taxes: *Boni pastoris est tondere pecus, non deglubere* ("A good shepherd shears his sheep, he doesn't flay them").

Social Cohesion

No man is an island. Society's economic difficulties eventually engulf even the most prosperous: *Tua res agitur, paries* cum *proximus ardet* ("You too are in danger when your neighbour's house is on fire").

Governance

In his novel *Pane e vino*[6] published in 1936, Ignazio Silone [1900–1978] explained how economic governance under the far right is a case of: "The government has one very long arm and one very short one. The long one is for taking, and reaches

[6] *Bread and Wine.*

everywhere, and the short one is for giving, but it only reaches those who are nearest".[7]

Virgil, in *The Aeneid*, compared governance to a sea voyage: *Per varios casus, per tot discrimina rerum* ("Through various misfortunes, and so many perils").

Seneca wrote: *Tranquillo. . .quilibet gubernator est* ("When it's calm. . . anybody can be the helmsman").

As underlined by the famous jurist Ulpian [170–223], who held the high office of Praetorian prefect: "Sometimes a term, though not expressed by its author, is implied in an act in the law, such as a contract or will. In that case the term is valid though the author does not add it, *etsi hoc non adiciat*".[8] This maxim should be borne in mind when expanding internationally, so as not to antagonise business partners and achieve sustainable, profitable growth.

In Book VI of *The Aeneid*, Anchise described thus the Roman way of governing: *Parcere subiectis et debellare superbos* ("To spare the humble and battle down the proud").

A medieval Latin saying goes: *Laedere facile, mederi difficile* ("Tis easier to hurt than heal").

As Plautus explained, motivation is crucial to succeed in an undertaking: *Stultitiast. . . venatum ducere invitas canes* ("It is foolishness to take unwilling dogs hunting").

As for Publilius Syrus: *Deliberandum est quicquid statuendum est semel* ("What is once resolved is to be long deliberated upon").

Seneca warned that: *Malignus comes quamvis candido et simplici robiginem suam affricat* ("An unkind companion will rub off his own rust on even the purest and most sincere soul").

Human Resources

Quintus Ennius [239–169 BC], often considered the father of Roman poetry, warned that: *Quem metuunt odere*: *quem quisque odit, periisse expetit* ("Whom men fear they hate, and whom they hate, they wish dead").

[7]Silone, Ignazio (1937, *Bread and Wine*, New York, London, Harper & Brothers Publishers.
[8]Honoré, Tony (1982), *Ulpian*, Oxford: Clarendon Press; New York: Oxford University Press.

Petronius [27–66 AD] wrote: *Qualis dominus talis et servus* ("Whatever kind of master, that is the kind of slave").

Gini Coefficient

Born in Motta di Livenza, Veneto, Corrado Gini [1884–1965] was an Italian statistician, demographer, ethnologist, and sociologist. The Gini coefficient was named after him.

A Gini coefficient normally has a value of between 0 (perfect equality-everyone has the same) and 1 (perfect inequality-one person has everything). The Gini, as it is also known, measures how far people are apart on average from perfect equality.

Money

In his *Epistles*, Horace warned: *Imperat aut servit collecta pecunia cuique* ("Money, as it increases, is either our master or our slave").

A proverb in medieval Latin made famous by Rabelais in *Gargantua et Pantagruel* states that: *Deficiente pecunia, deficit omne* ("It's all over when money is gone").

The Roman writer and courtier Petronius [c.27–66 AD], who was known as the *arbiter elegantiarum* (literally the "arbiter of refinements"), being the highest authority on manners and etiquette, and had the ear of Emperor Nero, wrote the following verse: *Quisquis habet nummos secura navigat aura* ("Whoever has money always sails with a safe wind").

Paradoxically, the more money you have, the more you want, as pointed out by Juvenal: *Crescit amor nummi, quantum ipsa pecunia crevit* ("The love of money increases as wealth itself increases").

Investment

In the play *Asinaria*, Plautus explained that you have to invest first to reap a profit: *Necesse est facere sumptum, qui quaerit lucrum* ("He who seeks profit must first make an expenditure").

Success

The epigram "You could criticize this more easily than you could imitate it", ascribed by Pliny to Zeuxis [464–398 BC], does express rather well the European attitude to success.

In his *Odes*, Horace warned that: *Feriuntque summos/fulgura montes* ("It is the mountain tops that the thunderbolts strike").

The same idea expressed by Publilius Syrus: *Excelsis multo facilius casus nocet* ("Fate more often harms them that be aloft").

Fall

Peter Chrysologus [380–450], the Bishop of Ravenna, considered that: "The higher you climb, the harder you fall".

Fortune

According to Publilius Syrus: *Fortuna vitrae est: tum* cum *splendet frangitur* ("Fortune is like glass: the brighter the glitter, the more easily broken").

Martial considered that: *Fortuna multis dat nimis, satis nulli* ("To many, fortune gives too much, to none enough").

Mergers and Acquisitions

When there is a merger and acquisition, the target may have developed such hard skills and corporate culture that the acquirer will end up being transformed and adopting these values. On these lines, Horace made the point that Greek culture conquered *Agresti Latio* ("rustic Latium"): *Graecia capta ferum victorem cepit* ("Once conquered, Greece conquered its conqueror").

In his *Satires*, Marcus Terentius Varro [116–27 AD] recalled that the strong prey upon the weak: *Piscem vorat maior minorem* ("Big fish eat little fish").

Establishment

In *Fasti*, Ovid stated: *In pretio pretium nunc est: dat census honores* ("Wealth is the value now: riches bring honours").

According to the poet, the door of the curia, as in a gathering of important men, remained closed to the poor.

Horace estimated that: *Principibus plaguisse vrisis non ultima laus est* ("It is not the least praise to have pleased leading men").

Reputation

According to Publilius Syrus: *Damnum appellandum est* cum *mala fama lucrum* ("Gain made at the expense of reputation must be reckoned as loss").

In his book *Scienza Nuova* published in 1744, Neapolitan philosopher and historian Giambattista Vico [1668–1744] wrote about the dynamics of reputation: *Fama crescit eundo* ("Reputation grows as it goes").

This synthesizes a famous passage from Virgil's *Aeneid* about reputation: "It flourishes by its very activity and gains new strength by its movements".

The *Aeneid* is an epic poem in 12 books, which Virgil started to write in 29 BC and never finished. He died, leaving a wish that the manuscript was to be burned. Emperor Augustus, however, ordered Virgil's literary executors to publish the poem with as few editorial changes as possible. Emperor Augustus [63–14 BC] named the eighth month of the year after himself, until then it was called Sextillis. Commonly repeated lore has it that August has 31 days because Augustus wanted his month to match July, named after Julius Caesar [100–44 BC].

Still in the *Aeneid*, Virgil wrote: *Fama malum quo non velocius ullum* ("Reputation: the report of evil things than which nothing is swifter").

Roman poet and satirist Aulus Persius Flaccus [34–62 AD] estimated that: *Pulchrum est digito monstrari et dicier, hic est* ("It is pleasant to be pointed at with the finger and to have it said, there he is").

For Ovid, money and honours are transient, only reputation is eternal. For this reason: *Omnia si perdas famam servare memento* ("If you lose everything, remember to keep your good name").

Aid

Publilius Syrus insisted that aid must be proffered rapidly in case of need: *Bis dat, qui dat celeriter* ("He who gives quickly gives twice").

Seneca warned that those we are obliged to are not necessarily our friends: *Leve aes alienum debitorem facit, grave inimicum* ("A trifling debt makes a man your debtor; a large one makes him an enemy").

Perseverance

The Roman poet and philosopher Lucretius [94–54 BC] reminds us of the effectiveness of perseverance and patience: *Gutta cavat lapidem* ("The drop hollows the stone").

In *De Agri Cultura*, Palladius (fourth century) explains that when work in the fields requires it, it is necessary to continue working without taking days off: *Necessitas feriis caret* ("Necessity knows no holiday").

As Seneca wrote, one must continue to do good in the face of another person's ingratitude: *Et post malam segetem serendum est* ("After a bad crop, immediately begin to sow").

This expression is often used as an invitation to persevere in the face of adversity.

A Latin expression says: *Patior ut potiar* ("I suffer that I may master").

Publilius Syrus warned against resting on one's laurels, for they wilt: *Laus nova nisi oritur, etiam vertus amittitur* ("If a new fame is not born, the old one also dies").

In *De Lege Agragria*, Cicero warns that no one is safe from the great temptation to rest after several victories before fighting the final battle, which requires mustering all one's strength. To succeed, you must press the enemy and fight one battle after another. He took the example of Hannibal who in 218, after wresting victory after victory from the Romans and the Battle of Cannae on 2 August 216 (which has become a classic in later military manuals) rested in Capua. As Cicero explained: *Hannibalem ispum Capua corrupit* ("Hannibal himself was corrupted by Capua").

Hannibal was everywhere victorious over the Romans. When he left Capua his star began to wane, and, though he did lay siege to Rome, he never breached the walls.

Any entrepreneur can vouch for the fact that, to succeed, you have to be prepared to put your shoulder to the wheel, never resting.

Driving Home an Advantage

In his book *Ab Urbe Condita*, in reference to the Battle of Cannae, Roman historian Livy [59 BC–17 AD] recalled the words of Maharbal, the Numidian army commander in charge of the cavalry under Hannibal: *Vincere scis, Hannibal, victoria uti nescis* ("You know how to win, Hannibal; you do not know how to use victory").

Timing

In his *Divus Augustus*, Suetonius deplored rashness in his military commanders, wanting them to act in a timely manner, calmly and sensibly: *Festina lente* ("Make haste slowly").

In his *Historiae Alexandri Magni*, Roman historian Quintus Curtius Rufus [first century] warned that foolishly rushing you risked tripping on your own heels: *Festinatio tarda est* ("Haste is already late").

According to Juvenal, listen to the voice of reason and caution for: *Galeatum sero duelli/paenitet* ("After donning the helmet, it is too late to repent of war").

Nevertheless, in his *Menaechmi*, Plautus emphasized that when danger rears its head a timely response is needed: *Folia nunc cadunt, praeut si triduom hoc hic erimus: tum arbores in te cadent* ("Mere leaves fall now, compared with what will be if we stay three days; then trees will fall on you").

In his *Tristia Ex Ponto*, Ovid explained that, in a desperate situation, when survival hangs in the balance, salvation is sought in ways that are no longer rational, but illusory: *Qui rapitur spumante salo, sua brachia tendens porrigit ad spinas duraque saxa manus* ("One who is being hurried along by the foaming sea stretches out his arms and grasps at thorns and hard rocks").

That is why it is so important to act before finding yourself in such a predicament.

This distich inspired several rather pithier sayings in English: "A drowning man will clutch at a straw", "A drowning man will grasp at straws"; and also "The drowning man clutches a serpent".

In his *Naturalis Historia,* Plinus the Eder [23–79 AD], who died in the eruption of Mount Vesuvius, insisted on the need for timeliness in all matters: "Grain sown at the right time often disappoints, but grain sown too late never betrays the worst expectations".

In the epic poem *Pharsalia* written by Lucan [39–65], Caius Curion urges Caesar to wait no more and cross the Rubicon: *Tolle moras: semper nocuit differre paratis* ("Make haste – delay has always harmed those who are prepared").

Adversity

Roman soldier and historian Ammianus Marcellinus recalled that beauty flourishes even in the midst of adversity: *Inter vepres rosae nascuntur* ("Roses are born among thorns").

In the *Metamorphoses*, Ovid pointed out that: *Fas est et ab hoste doceri* ("One should learn even from one's enemies").

A medieval proverb invites us to reflect on how we deal with adversity: "Who makes himself a sheep will be eaten by the wolves".

Dominant Country

Nowadays, when taking about the dominant power, any references are to the United States, not Washington. When the Roman Empire was the world's leading power, all references were to Rome.

Emperor Diocletian [244–311 AD], who ruled from 284 to 305 AD, had the following inscription engraved on his crown: *Caput mundi regit orbis frena rotundi* ("The capital of the world holds the reins of the Earth's orb").

Roma aeterna ("Rome eternal") described a city that, at the time, acted as a beacon for the world.

Strategy

In *Ars Amatoria*, Ovid explained that: "He is a foolish swimmer who swims against the stream".

Monetary Policy Announcements

Central bank monetary policy announcements, in that they contain commitments regarding future decisions, form part of a strategy for managing the expectations of economic agents. They are part of the unconventional monetary policy instruments, alongside the supply of liquidity, asset purchase programmes, and quantitative easing.

In July 2012, during the sovereign debt crisis, to restore market confidence, Mario Draghi [1947–], the President of the European Central Bank from 2011 to 2019, stated: "Within our mandate, the ECB is ready to do whatever it takes to preserve the euro. And believe me, it will be enough".[9]

Shortly after, the European Central Bank (ECB) went on to announce a new programme of open-ended, unlimited buying of government bonds, what it termed outright monetary transactions, but it was never activated as Mario Draghi's intervention had instantly restored confidence.

Fascism

The institutional dynamics that propelled fascism to power in Italy and Germany are little studied or taught today. On 25 April 1995, to mark the 50th anniversary of the Liberation of Italy, Umberto Eco [1932–2016] gave a lecture at Columbia University, entitled *Ur-Fascism,*[10] in which he criticised aspects of society (popular elitism, machismo, rejection of analytical criticism, use of an impoverished vocabulary and an elementary syntax to limit complex and critical reasoning) that harked back to fascism.

Umberto Eco's view was that: "Mussolini did not have any philosophy: he had only rhetoric".

In his speech, Umberto Eco attempted to outline the features that are typical of what he called Ur-Fascism, or Eternal Fascism, explaining that: "These features cannot be organised into a system; many of them contradict each other, and are also typical of other kinds of despotism or fanaticism. But it is enough that one of them be present to allow fascism to coagulate around it".

---

[9] Video: https://www.youtube.com/watch?v=W97hM8eCE5g

[10] Eco, Umberto (1995), *Ur-Fascism*, http://www.nybooks.com/articles/1995/06/22/ur-fascism/ Also https://sites.evergreen.edu/politicalshakespeares/wp-content/uploads/sites/226/2015/12/Eco-urfascism.pdf

He listed 14 such features:

1. The first feature of Ur-Fascism is the *cult of tradition.* [. . .]
2. Traditionalism implies the *rejection of modernism.* [. . .] In this sense Ur-Fascism can be defined as *irrationalism.* [. . .]
3. Irrationalism also depends on the cult of *action for action's sake.* [. . .] Thinking is a form of emasculation. Therefore, culture is suspect insofar as it is identified with critical attitudes. [. . .]
4. For Ur-Fascism, disagreement is treason. [. . .]
5. *Fear of difference* [. . .]
6. Ur-Fascism derives from *individual or social frustration.* That is why one of the most typical features of the historical fascism was the *appeal to a frustrated middle class*, a class suffering from an economic crisis or feelings of political humiliation, and frightened by the pressure of lower social groups. [. . .]
7. *Nationalism* [. . .]

Umberto Eco went on:

8. *Enemies are at the same time too strong and too weak.* [. . .]
9. *Pacifism is trafficking with the enemy.* It is bad because *life is permanent warfare.* [. . .] there must be a final battle, after which the movement will have control of the world. But such a 'final solution' implies a further era of peace, a Golden Age, which contradicts the principle of permanent war. [. . .]
10. *Contempt for the weak.* [. . .] Since the group is hierarchically organized (according to a military model), every subordinate leader despises his own underlings, and each of them despises his inferiors. This reinforces the sense of mass elitism. [. . .]
11. In such a perspective *everybody is educated to become a hero.* [. . .]
12. *Machismo.* [. . .]
13. For Ur-Fascism [. . .] individuals as individuals have no rights, and the People is conceived as a quality, a monolithic entity expressing the Common Will. [. . .] There is in our future a *TV or Internet populism*, in which the emotional response of a selected group of citizens can be presented and accepted as the Voice of the People.
14. All the Nazi or Fascist schoolbooks made use of an impoverished vocabulary, and an elementary syntax, in order to limit the instruments for complex and critical reasoning.[11]

[11] Eco, Umberto (1995), *Ur-Fascism*, http://www.nybooks.com/articles/1995/06/22/ur-fascism/ Also https://sites.evergreen.edu/politicalshakespeares/wp-content/uploads/sites/226/2015/12/Eco-urfascism.pdf

United Kingdom

Money Supply

The philosopher Francis Bacon [1561–1626] considered that money must circulate to be beneficial to the economy: "Above all things, good policy is to be used, that the treasure and moneys, in a state, be not gathered into few hands. For otherwise a state may have a great stock, and yet starve. And money is like muck, not good except it be spread".[1]

As explained by David Hume [1711–1776] in his 1752 essay *Of Money*: "It is the oil which renders the motion of the wheels more smooth and easy".[2]

In the *Principles of Political Economy* published in 1848, John Stuart Mill [1806–1873] explained that: "The value of money will depend upon its quantity, together with the average number of times that each piece changes hands in the process. [...] the amount of goods and of transactions being the same, the value of money is inversely as its quantity multiplied by what is called the rapidity of circulation".[3]

Money

An English proverb states that: "Money is round, so it has to roll".

---

[1] Bacon, Francis (1625), *Of Seditions and Troubles*, http://www.esp.org/books/bacon/essays/contents/essay15.pdf

[2] Hume, David (1752), Of Money, https://davidhume.org/texts/pld/mo

[3] Mill, John Stuart (1885), *Principles of Political Economy*, from The Project Gutenberg EBook of Principles Of Political Economy by John Stuart Mill.

C. Peicuti, *The European Economy in 100 Quotes*, Contributions to Economics,
https://doi.org/10.1007/978-3-031-68819-5_4

In *Timon of Athens*, William Shakespeare [1564–1616] sees money as a facilitator: "His large fortune, upon his good and gracious nature hanging, subdues".

Capital

Adam Smith [1723–1790] warned about the mobility of capital, which facilitates its flight when economic or fiscal conditions deteriorate: "A merchant, it has been said very properly, is not necessarily the citizen of any particular country. It is in a great measure indifferent to him from what place he carries on his trade; and a very trifling disgust will make him remove his capital, and together with it all the industry which it supports, from one country to another".[4]

Savings

In *Towards a Dynamic Economics* published in 1948, Roy Forbes Harrod [1900–1978] explained that: "Saving is a virtue and [...] a force making for depression".[5]

Unemployment

In his magnum opus, *The General Theory of Employment, Interest and Money*, published in late 1936, John Maynard Keynes [1883–1946] explained that: "The evidence indicates that full, or even approximately full, employment is of rare and short-lived occurrence". But then, on the other hand, that: "Unemployment feeds upon itself, each increment to unemployment begetting further unemployment", as a man losing his job will increase unemployment among workers that would have produced the good that he no longer has the means to purchase, leading to a vicious circle.

In *The Theory of Unemployment* published in 1930, Arthur Cécil Pigou [1877–1959] explained that: "Unemployment as exists at any time is due wholly to the fact that changes in demand conditions are continually taking place and that

[4] Smith, Adam (1776), *An Inquiry into the Nature and Causes of the Wealth of Nations*, https://www.ibiblio.org/ml/libri/s/SmithA_WealthNations_p.pdf

[5] Harrod, Roy Forbes (1948), *Towards A Dynamic Economics, Some Recent Developments of Economic Theory and their Application to Policy*, London: Macmillan & Co, Ltd., http://tankona.free.fr/harrod1948.pdf

frictional resistances prevent the appropriate wage adjustments from being made instantaneously".[6]

He adds that: "There will always be at work a strong tendency for wage-rates to be so related to demand that everybody is employed. Hence, in stable conditions everyone will actually be employed".[7]

Economic System

As Jeremy Bentham (1748–1832) remarked with great humour in *A Despot's Interest in the Prosperity of his Subjects*: "It is the interest of the wolf that the sheep should be fat and abundant".

As explained by Alfred Marshall [1842–1924] in *Principles of Economics* published in 1890: "Other things being equal, one person has more real wealth in its broadest sense than another, if the place in which the former lives has a better climate, better roads, better water, more wholesome drainage; and again better newspapers, books, and places of amusement and instruction".[8]

In the speech given by Tony Blair [1953–] to the European Parliament in Brussels on 23 June 2005, about the role of the social model in a global economy, the British Prime Minister said: "The purpose of our social model should be to enhance our ability to compete, to help our people cope with globalization, to let them embrace its opportunities and avoid its dangers".[9]

Consumer

Adam Smith estimated that: "Consumption is the sole end and purpose of all production; and the interest of the producer ought to be attended to, only so far as it may be necessary for promoting that of the consumer".[10]

---

[6] Pigou, Arthur Cécil (1933), *The Theory of Unemployment*, MacMillan & Co., Limited.

[7] Ibid.

[8] Marshall, Alfred (1961), *Principles of Economics*, Ninth (variorum) Edition with annotations by C.W. Guillebaud, Volume 1, Macmillan & Co. Ltd., Royal Economic Society.

[9] http://edition.cnn.com/2005/WORLD/europe/06/23/blair.europe.text/index.html

[10] Smith, Adam (1776), *An Inquiry into the Nature and Causes of the Wealth of Nations.*

Trade Exchanges

In *An Inquiry into the Nature and Causes of the Wealth of Nations* published in 1776, Adam Smith identified trade exchanges as the quintessence of the market economy: "Every man thus lives by exchanging, or becomes in some measure a merchant, and the society itself grows to be what is properly a commercial society".[11]

Crisis

David Ricardo [1772–1823] explained: "The commencement of war after a long peace, or of peace after a long war, generally produces considerable distress in trade. It changes in a great degree the nature of the employments to which the respective capitals of countries were before devoted; and during the interval while they are settling in the situations which new circumstances have made the most beneficial, much-fixed capital is unemployed, perhaps wholly lost, and labourers are without full employment. The duration of this distress will be longer or shorter according to the strength of that disinclination which most men feel to abandon that employment of their capital to which they have long been accustomed".[12]

Demography

In *An Inquiry into the Nature and Causes of the Wealth of Nations*, Adam Smith considered that: "The most decisive mark of the prosperity of any country is the increase of the number of its inhabitants".

Thomas Malthus [1766–1834], in *An Essay on the Principle of Population*, warned that: "Population, when unchecked, increases in a geometrical ratio. Subsistence increases only in an arithmetical ratio. A slight acquaintance with numbers will show the immensity of the first power in comparison of the second".[13]

[11] Ibid.

[12] Ricardo, David (1817), *On the Principles of Political Economy and Taxation*, third edition 1821, Batoche Books, Kitchener.

[13] Malthus, Thomas (1798), *An Essay on the Principle of Population*, London, Printed for J. Johnson, in St. Paul's Church-Yard.

Debt

In her address to the Conservative Party Conference in 1983, Prime Minister Margaret Thatcher [1925–2013] stressed that: "There is no such thing as public money, there is only taxpayers' money". As she explained: "If the state wishes to spend more, it can do so only by borrowing your savings or by taxing you more".

Entrepreneur

Winston Churchill [1874–1965] saw the entrepreneur as the engine of growth: "Among our Socialist opponents there is great confusion. Some of them regard private enterprise as a predatory tiger to be shot. Others look on it as a cow they can milk. Only a handful see it for what it really is - the strong and willing horse that pulls the whole cart along".[14]

Value

In the *Principles of Political Economy* published in 1848, John Stuart Mill explained that: "The value of a thing in any place depends on the cost of its acquisition in that place; which, in the case of an imported article, means the cost of production of the thing which is exported to pay for it".[15]

Poverty

John Stuart Mill wondered how to help the poor without making them dependent on aid, and enabling them to emerge from poverty: "The problem to be solved is therefore one of peculiar nicety as well as importance; how to give the greatest amount of needful help, with the smallest encouragement to undue reliance on it".[16]

Thomas Malthus also stressed the difficulty of rescuing the poor from poverty instead of condemning them to this condition in perpetuity: "To remedy the frequent

[14]Churchill, Winston, from Langsworth, Richard (2008, 2012, 2016), *Churchill by Himself: The Definitive Book of Quotations.*

[15]Mill, John Stuart (1885), *Principles of Political Economy*, from The Project Gutenberg EBook of Principles Of Political Economy by John Stuart Mill.

[16]Mill, John Stuart (1848), *Principles of Political Economy*, from The Project Gutenberg EBook of Principles Of Political Economy by John Stuart Mill.

distresses of the common people, the poor laws of England have been instituted; but it is to be feared, that though they may have alleviated a little the intensity of individual misfortune, they have spread the general evil over a much larger surface".[17]

In *The Great Escape: Health, Wealth, and the Origins of Inequality* published in 2013, Angus Deaton [1945–], who was awarded the 2015 Nobel Prize for Economic Sciences, wrote: "As we already know from the poverty numbers, the bottom fifth of families gained very little. The growth in their average incomes was less than 0.2 percent a year over the past forty-four years and, even before the recession, their real incomes were no higher than they had been in the late 1970s. Average incomes of the top fifth, by contrast, grew more quickly, at 1.6 percent a year, though not as quickly as those of the top 5 percent, whose average incomes grew at 2.1 percent a year".[18]

Deaton denounces the failure of many regions to "escape" the "horrors of destitution and of premature death", making the point that: "If poverty is not a result of lack of resources or opportunities, but of poor institutions, poor government, and toxic politics, giving money to poor countries - particularly giving money to the governments of poor countries - is likely to perpetuate and prolong poverty, not eliminate it".[19]

Monopoly

Adam Smith is against monopolies, explaining that: "To promote the little interest of one little order of men in one country, [the monopoly] hurts the interest of all other orders of men in that country, and of all men in all other countries".[20]

Productivity

The economist Alfred Marshall explained that: "It may be possible for an increase in the population to cause a more than proportional increase in the means of subsistence",[21] adding that: "We can say broadly that while the part which nature plays in

---

[17] Malthus, Thomas (1798), *An Essay on the Principle of Population*, London, Printed for J. Johnson, in St. Paul's Church-Yard.

[18] Deaton, Angus (2013), *The Great Escape: Health, Wealth, and the Origins of Inequality*, Princeton University Press, Princeton and Oxford.

[19] Ibid.

[20] Smith, Adam (1776), *An Inquiry into the Nature and Causes of the Wealth of Nations*, from https://www.ibiblio.org/ml/libri/s/SmithA_WealthNations_p.pdf

[21] Marshall, Alfred (1961), *Principles of Economics*, Ninth (variorum) Edition with annotations by C.W. Guillebaud, Volume 1, Macmillan & Co. Ltd., Royal Economic Society.

production shows a tendency to diminishing return, the part which man plays shows a tendency to increasing return".[22]

Speculation

When the stock market no longer reflects the intrinsic value of companies, but drives up their values, triggering a speculative spiral, a bubble forms. It will eventually burst, leading to a correction in the share prices of the companies directly concerned, but also causing collateral damage as we saw with the subprime bubble. Keynes summed it up as follows: "Speculators may do no harm as bubbles on a steady stream of enterprise. But the position is serious when enterprise becomes the bubble on a whirlpool of speculation".[23]

Growth

As explained by John Stuart Mill in *Principles of Political Economy* published in 1848: "The increase of wealth is not boundless; that at the end of what they term the progressive state lies the stationary state [...]. The richest and most prosperous countries would very soon attain the stationary state, if no further improvements were made in the productive arts"[24] or if there is no increase in the effective desire for accumulation.

Jump the Curve published in 2008 contains the following comment by Kenneth Ewart Boulding [1910–1993]: "Anyone who believes exponential growth can go on forever in a finite world is either a madman or an economist".

Angus Deaton considers that: "Life is a great escape from deprivation and early death". He explains that nothing guarantees there is a general relationship between growth and poverty unless Nation-States intervene in the redistribution of wealth in their country. For the British economist, progress in this area is non-linear. There being no world government to act on international inequalities, inequality between individuals will continue at the level of the planet. Deaton highlights the fact that there are almost unimaginable differences between countries in the average material standard of living and that the gap between the poor and the rich within each country

[22] Ibid.

[23] Keynes, John Maynard (1936), *The General Theory of Employment, Interest, and Money*, from https://www.files.ethz.ch/isn/125515/1366_keynestheoryofemployment.pdf

[24] Mill, John Stuart (1885), *Principles of Political Economy*, from The Project Gutenberg EBook of Principles Of Political Economy by John Stuart Mill.

is only slightly smaller. He warns that income inequality in many rich countries has soared in recent years.

What has been observed by Deaton is a positive correlation between life expectancy and income: in other words, health and wealth often go hand in hand.

Deaton considers that: "Averages are no consolation to those who have been left behind" and that "Economic growth has been the engine of international income inequality".

Wellbeing

Deaton draws our attention to the fact that: "Economists focus on income, public health scholars focus on mortality and morbidity, and demographers focus on births, deaths, and the size of populations. All of these factors contribute to wellbeing, but none of them is wellbeing".

He adds: "To worry about these consequences of extreme inequality has nothing to do with being envious of the rich and everything to with the fear that rapidly growing top incomes are a threat to the wellbeing of everyone else".

His view is that: "GDP omits much that is central to people's wellbeing", in addition to which it also has its limitations as a measure of income.

Gross Domestic Product

According to Angus Deaton: "Material wellbeing and measures of it-GDP, personal income, and consumption-have recently received a bad press. Spending more, we are often told, does not bring us better lives, and religious authorities regularly warn against materialism. Even among those of us who endorse economic growth, there are many critics of GDP as it is currently defined and measured. GDP excludes important activities, such as services by homemakers; it takes no account of leisure; and it often does a poor job of measuring those things that are included. It also includes things that arguably should be excluded, like the cost of cleaning up pollution or building prisons or commuting. These 'defensive' expenditures are not good in and of themselves but are regrettably necessary to enable things that are good".

He adds: "If crime goes up, and we spend more on prisons, GDP will be higher. If we neglect climate change, and spend more and more on cleaning up and repairing after storms, GDP will go up, not down; we count the repairs but ignore the destruction".

Inequalities

Deaton estimates that: "It can be bad if the winners try to stop others from following them, pulling up the ladders behind them".

For John Stuart Mill: "The best state for human nature is that in which, while no one is poor, no one desires to be richer, nor has any reason to fear being thrust back, by the efforts of others to push themselves forward. I know not why it should be matter of congratulation that persons who are already richer than any one needs to be, should have doubled their means of consuming things which give little or no pleasure except as representative of wealth".[25]

And he went on: "As little is there an inherent necessity that any human being should be a selfish egotist".[26]

In *Deaths of Despair and the Future of Capitalism* published in 2021, Anne Case [1958–], the Alexander Stewart 1886 Professor of Economics and Public Affairs, emeritus, at Princeton University, and Angus Deaton wrote that, even though COVID-19 was receding, the surge in "deaths of despair" (which is how the authors characterised fatalities from drugs, suicide, and alcohol) amongst the white working-class Americans, who had believed in the American dream, would continue. The authors attribute this phenomenon to precarious employment and the uberisation of labour relations, the resulting distress being dulled by the consumption of drugs and alcohol.

They draw attention to the fact that, for the first time since 1918, life expectancy in the United States has fallen for 3 years in a row.

For the authors: "Inequality is much cited for its baleful impacts. [...] We see inequality as a consequence as much as a cause; if the rich are allowed to enrich themselves through unfair processes that hold down wages, and raise prices, then inequality will certainly rise. But not everyone gets rich that way. Some people invent new tools, drugs, or gadgets, or new ways of doing things, and benefit many, not just themselves. They profit from improving and extending other people's lives.

---

[25] Mill, John Stuart (1848), *Principles of Political Economy*, Book IV, Chap. VI, http://gesd.free.fr/millst.pdf

[26] Mill, John Stuart, *Utilitarianism, Liberty & Representation*, https://ia803401.us.archive.org/11/items/utilitarianismli0000mill_t8w5/utilitarianismli0000mill_t8w5.pdf

It is good for great innovators to get rich. Making is not the same as taking. It is not inequality itself that is unfair but rather the process that generates it".

Economist

Keynes defined the economist as follows: "The master-economist must possess a rare combination of gifts. He must reach a high standard in several different directions and must combine talents not often found together. He must be mathematician, historian, statesman, philosopher - in some degree. He must understand symbols and speak in words. He must contemplate the particular in terms of the general, and touch abstract and concrete in the same flight of thought. He must study the present in the light of the past for the purposes of the future. No part of man's nature or his institutions must lie entirely outside his regard. He must be purposeful and disinterested in a simultaneous mood, as aloof and incorruptible as an artist, yet sometimes as near the earth as a politician".[27]

Wages

In *An Inquiry into the Nature and Causes of the Wealth of Nations*, Adam Smith insisted on the importance of fair pay: "The liberal reward of labour, as it encourages the propagation, so it increases the industry of the common people. The wages of labour are the encouragement of industry, which, like every other human quality, improves in proportion to the encouragement it receives".[28]

The 1972 Sveriges Riksbank Prize in Economic Sciences in Memory of Alfred Nobel was awarded jointly to British economist John Hicks [1904–1989] and American economist Kenneth Arrow [1921–2017] "for their pioneering contributions to general economic equilibrium theory and welfare theory". Paul Samuelson considers Hicks to be the "father of modern microeconomics".

The Theory of Wages published in 1932 is a classic microeconomic statement of wage determination. According to the British economist: "The theory of the determination of wages in a free market is simply a special case of the general theory of value. Wages are the price of labour".[29]

---

[27] Keynes, John Maynard (1933), *Essays In Biography*, MacMillan and Co. from https://archive.org/details/in.ernet.dli.2015.536827/page/n1/mode/2up

[28] Smith, Adam (1776), *An Inquiry into the Nature and Causes of the Wealth of Nations*, from https://www.ibiblio.org/ml/libri/s/SmithA_WealthNations_p.pdf

[29] Hicks, John (1932), *The Theory of Wages*, second edition 1963, Palgrave Macmillan.

In *Value and Capital* published in 1939, he stated: "The purpose of income calculations in practical affairs is to give people an indication of how much they can consume without impoverishing themselves. Following out this idea, it would seem that we ought to define a man's income as the maximum value which he can consume during a week, and still expect to be as well off at the end of the week as he was at the beginning".[30]

Needs

In *Principles of Economics* published in 1890, Alfred Marshall wrote: "There seems to be no good reason for believing that we are anywhere near a stationary state in which there will be no new important wants to be satisfied [...]. The whole history of man shows that his wants expand with the growth of his wealth and knowledge".[31]

Nevertheless for Marshall: "The total utility of a thing to anyone [...] increase with every increase in his stock of it, but not as fast as his stock increases. If his stock of it increases at a uniform rate the benefit derived from it increases at a diminishing rate".[32]

Investment

For John Stuart Mill: "As the wages of the labourer are the remuneration of labour, so the profits of the capitalist are properly, according to Mr. Senior's well-chosen expression, the remuneration of abstinence. They are what he gains by forbearing to consume his capital for his own uses, and allowing it to be consumed by productive labourers for their uses. For this forbearance he requires a recompense".[33]

According to Hicks: "Investment is a flighty bird which needs to be controlled".

[30] Hicks, John (1939), *Value and Capital, An Inquiry into some Fundamental Principles of Economic Theory*, second edition 1946, Oxford at the Clarendon Press.

[31] Marshall, Alfred (1961), *Principles of Economics*, Ninth (variorum) Edition with annotations by C.W. Guillebaud, Volume 1, Macmillan & Co. Ltd., Royal Economic Society.

[32] Ibid.

[33] Mill, John Stuart (1848), *Principles of Political Economy*, from The Project Gutenberg EBook of Principles Of Political Economy by John Stuart Mill.

Central Bank

One consequence of the wars between England and France was the creation of the Bank of England in 1694 in London. In December 1693, the government of William III needed "the summe of Fifteene hundred thousand pounds towards the carrying on the War against France".[34]

To this end, based on a proposal by William Paterson made in 1691, the so-called Tonnage Act was passed in 1694, buried in which was an authorisation to subscribe this great public loan, in return for which the subscriber would be incorporated as the Governor and Company of the Bank of England. The operation was a success, with the amount paid over to the Exchequer in the form of notes bearing the Bank of England's seal.

For Hicks: "Only in a national economy that is largely self-contained can a national central bank be a true central bank; with the development of world market, and (especially) of world financial markets, national central banks take a step down, becoming single banks in a worldwide system, not at the 'centre' any longer. Thus the problem that was (partially) solved by the institution of national central banks has reappeared, and it is still unsolved (though we are trying to solve it), on the world level".[35]

In *Principles of Political Economy and Taxation*, David Ricardo drew attention to the fact that: "Experience, however, shows that neither a state nor a bank ever have had the unrestricted power of issuing paper money without abusing that power; in all states, therefore, the issue of paper money ought to be under some check and control; and none seems so proper for that purpose as that of subjecting the issuers of paper money to the obligation of paying their notes either in gold coin or bullion". What would the British economist have to say about monetary policy in the twenty-first century?

In *The Art of Central Banking* published in 1932, Ralph George Hawtrey [1879–1975] wrote: "Rarely does a policy of cheap money fail to start a revival".

---

[34] Bank of England Act 1694, https://www.legislation.gov.uk/aep/WillandMar/5-6/20/section/XXVI

[35] Hicks, John (1967), *The Two Triads*, in Collected Essays in Monetary Theory, Oxford: Clarendon Press.

Auto Economy

John Hicks explained that, in the case of the auto economy, borrowers approach economic agents with financing capacity directly via the financial markets. Businesses (what he calls "merchants") raise their financing directly on the market, with borrowings from the banking system playing only a limited role. The credit multiplier is at work. Banks can only create scriptural money in proportion to the monetary base.

Overdraft Economy

In the overdraft economy, a term coined by John Hicks, financing is indirect via financial intermediaries positioned between investors and savers. In this type of economy, financing is mainly by bank credit. Financial markets play a marginal role. For John Hicks, although this system enables issuers of securities with insufficient reputation to obtain financing and enables savers to reduce their risk thanks to the intervention of experts, it is at the origin of a double indebtedness: that of companies to commercial banks and that of commercial banks to the Central Bank. Few banks still have enough cash on hand to engage in financial intermediation. As the central bank's monetary policy is dominated by the desire to support growth, commercial banks are guaranteed almost automatic refinancing. In this case, the credit divider is at work. John Hicks highlights the fact that in such circumstances the central bank is subject to the decisions of the commercial banks, which require it to issue money in proportion to their own financing needs.

Contractual Incompleteness

In *Firms, Contracts, and Financial Structure,* Oliver Hart [1948–], who shared the 1972 Sveriges Riksbank Prize in Economic Sciences in Memory of Alfred Nobel with Finnish economist Bengt Holmström [1949-] "for their contributions to contract theory", explains why contractual incompleteness matters: "The reason is that the renegotiation process imposes several costs. Some of these are ex post costs, incurred at the renegotiation stage itself, and others are ex ante costs, incurred in anticipation of renegotiation".[36]

[36]Hart, Oliver (1995), *Firms, Contracts, and Financial Structure*, Clarendon Press.

Data

Ronald H. Coase [1910–2013] was awarded the 1991 Sveriges Riksbank Prize in Economic Sciences in Memory of Alfred Nobel "for his discovery and clarification of the significance of transaction costs and property rights for the institutional structure and functioning of the economy".

According to the British economist and author: "If you torture the data long enough, it will confess".

He also explained that: "Data can't speak for itself; it's up to you to give it a voice. Try to speak truthfully".

Regulation

Ronald H. Coase stated: "I can't remember one [example of regulation] that's good. Regulation of transport, regulation of agriculture - agriculture is a, zoning is z. You know, you go from a to z, they are all bad. There were so many studies, and the result was quite universal: The effects were bad".

Economic Science

As explained by Ronald H. Coase: "Economics, over the years, has become more and more abstract and divorced from events in the real world. Economists, by and large, do not study the workings of the actual economic system. They theorize about it. As Ely Devons, an English economist, once said at a meeting, "If economists wished to study the horse, they wouldn't go and look at horses. They'd sit in their studies and say to themselves, 'What would I do if I were a horse?'"[37]

He added: "In my youth it was said that what was too silly to be said may be sung. In modern economics it may be put into mathematics".[38]

Also that: "The tools used by economists to analyze business firms are too abstract and speculative to offer any guidance to entrepreneurs and managers in their constant struggle to bring novel products to consumers at low cost".[39]

---

[37] Coase, Ronald H. (1999), *Speech to ISNIE: The Task of the Society*, https://www.coase.org/coasespeech.htm

[38] Coase, Ronald H. (1988), *The Firm, the Market, and the Law*, University of Chicago Press, Chicago.

[39] Coase, Ronald H. (2012), *Saving Economics from the Economists*, Harvard Business Review.

He warned that: "Economics as currently presented in textbooks and taught in the classroom does not have much to do with business management, and still less with entrepreneurship".[40]

He explained that globalisation and the increasing complexity of the modern economy meant exhaustive economic analyses were impossible: "The time has surely gone in which economists could analyze in great detail two individuals exchanging nuts for berries on the edge of the forest and then feel that their analysis of the process of exchange was complete, illuminating though this analysis may be in certain respects".[41]

Saving

According to Winston Churchill: "Saving is a fine thing. Especially when your parents have done it for you".

Decision-Making

Ronald H. Coase stated: "We must first note that economic factors are taken into account in a world in which ignorance, prejudice, and mental confusion, encouraged rather than dispelled by the political organization, exert a strong influence on policy making".[42]

Enterprise

For Ronald H. Coase: "A firm [...] consists of the system of relationships which comes into existence when the direction of resources is dependent on an entrepreneur. As a firm gets larger, there may be decreasing returns to the entrepreneur function, that is, the costs of organizing additional transactions within the firm may rise".[43]

---

[40] Ibid.

[41] Coase, Ronald H. (1988), *The Firm, the Market, and the Law*, University of Chicago Press, Chicago.

[42] Coase, Ronald H. (1966), *The Economics of Broadcasting and Government Policy*, The American Economic Review, Vol. 56, No. 1/2 (Mar. 1, 1966), pp. 440–447, American Economic Association.

[43] Coase, Ronald H. (1937), *The Nature of the Firm*, Economica LSE.

He considered: "Changes like the telephone and telegraphy, which tend to reduce the cost of organizing spatially, will tend to increase the size of the firm".[44]

In *Value and Capital* published in 1965, Hicks explained that: "It [the enterprise] acquires factors, and sells products; its aim is to maximize the difference between their value".[45]

Property

In the *Second Treatise of Civil Government* published in 1690, John Locke [1632–1704] observed: "The great and chief end, therefore, of men's uniting into commonwealths, and putting themselves under government, is the preservation of their property".

In the *Second Treatise of Civil Government*, John Locke explained that the land and what is the labour of his body, and the work of his hands is an extension of man himself, and as a man belongs to himself, any extension must also be properly his.

Coase points out that: "The law of property determines who owns something, but the market determines how it will be used".

Economic Theory

In *Essays on Economics and Economists* published in 1994, Ronald H. Coase writes: "But a theory is not like an airline or bus timetable. We are not interested simply in the accuracy of its predictions. A theory also serves as a base for thinking. It helps us to understand what is going on by enabling us to organize our thoughts. Faced with a choice between a theory which predicts well but gives us little insight into how the system works and one which gives us this insight but predicts badly, I would choose the latter, and I am inclined to think that most economists would do the same".[46]

---

[44]Coase, Ronald H. (1988), *The Firm, the Market, and the Law*, University of Chicago Press, Chicago.

[45]Hicks, John (1978), *Value and Capital, An Inquiry into some Fundamentals Principles of Economic Theory*, Oxford, Clarendon Press.

[46]Coase, Ronald H. (1995), *Essays on Economics and Economists*, University of Chicago Press, Chicago.

State

In *Of the Independency of Parliament* published in 1777, David Hume has these words of advice: "Every man ought to be supposed a knave, and to have no other end, in all his actions, than private interest. By this interest we must govern him, and, by means of it, make him, notwithstanding his insatiable avarice and ambition, co-operate to public good".[47]

Ronald H. Coase warns against excessive state interference: "An important reason may be that government at the present time is so large that it has reached the stage of negative marginal productivity, which means that any additional function it takes on will probably result in more harm than good.... If a federal program were established to give financial assistance to Boy Scouts to enable them to help old ladies cross busy intersections, we could be sure that not all the money would go to Boy Scouts, that some of those they helped would be neither old nor ladies, that part of the program would be devoted to preventing old ladies from crossing busy intersections, and that many of them would be killed because they would now cross at places where, unsupervised, they were at least permitted to cross".

Behavioural Analysis

In *The Firm, the Market, and the Law*, Ronald H. Coase wrote: "I believe that human preferences came to be what they are in those millions of years in which our ancestors (whether or not they can be classified as human) lived in hunting bands and were those preferences which, in such conditions, were conducive to survival. It may be, therefore, that ultimately the work of sociobiologists (and their critics) will enable us to construct a picture of human nature in such detail that we can derive the set of preferences with which economists start. And if this result is achieved, it will enable us to refine our analysis of consumer demand and of other kinds of behaviour in the economic sphere".

Socialism

Winston Churchill delivered this analysis of socialism: "Christopher Columbus was the first socialist: he didn't know where he was going, he didn't know where he was? And he did it all at taxpayers' expense".

---

[47] Hume, David (1777), *Of the Independency of Parliament*, Essays Moral, Political, and Literary, Edited and with a Foreword, Notes, and Glossary by Eugene E Miller, https://oll-resources.s3.us-east-2.amazonaws.com/oll3/store/titles/704/0059_Bk.pdf

He added: "It is a socialist idea that making profits is a vice. I consider the real vice is making losses".

In her book *The Downing Street Years* published in 1993, Margaret Thatcher wrote: "The unspoken objective of socialism [...] was to increase dependency. Poverty was not just the breeding ground of socialism: it was the deliberately engineered effect of it".[48]

Prices

In *On the Principles of Political Economy and Taxation* published in 1817, David Ricardo explained that: "It is the cost of production which must ultimately regulate the price of commodities"; and that: "Possessing utility, commodities derive their exchangeable value from two sources: from their scarcity, and from the quantity of labour required to obtain them".[49]

Innovation

As underlined by John Stuart Mill in 1848: "Genius can only breathe freely in an atmosphere of freedom".[50]

Success

Anthony Trollope (1815–1882) warned against the harmful effects of premature success: "Success is a poison that should only be taken late in life and then only in small doses".

[48] Thatcher, Margaret (1993), *The Downing Street Years*, London: HarperCollins.

[49] Ricardo, David (1817), *On the Principles of Political Economy and Taxation*, London: John Murray, Albemarle-Street, https://www.gutenberg.org/cache/epub/33310/pg33310-images.html

[50] Mill, John Stuart (1859), *On Liberty*, The Walter Scott Publishing Co., Ltd., London and Felling-on-Tyne New York and Melbourne, from The Project Gutenberg eBook of On Liberty.

France

After the Romans conquered much of Europe and attempted to fashion it into an economic and political entity where all roads led to Rome, the idea of a European economic federation began to emerge amongst French economists and politicians as early as the Renaissance, when ancient Europe rose from the ashes. At that time, the unity of European civilisation was already self-evident.

As this period was followed by the long reign of Louis XIV [1638–1715] from 1643 to 1715, French economic ideas gained worldwide recognition. Later, it would be British, and then American economic ideas that would take over for centuries.

One thousand years after Charlemagne, King of the Franks from 768, crowned Emperor of the Romans in 800, Napoleon [1769–1821] cherished the dream of treading in the steps of the Roman emperors after Constantine the Great [272–337]. The royal regalia used for the coronation included the Crown of Charlemagne, adorned with jewels borrowed from the Cathedral of Aix-la-Chapelle built by Charlemagne based on a multiple of 12, like the number of stars on the European Union flag. To everyone's astonishment, after his coronation, Napoleon returned the jewels to the cathedral.

However, his dream of centralising Europe under the aegis of France was not shared by his contemporaries. The protagonists of the French Revolution, including Talleyrand, dreamt of a Europe that would be fraternal. In the 26 August 1790 edition of the *Moniteur*, Mirabeau [1749–1791] declared: "We look forward to a time when [...] Europe will form one great family, for then the pact to federate humankind will be consummated".

It was their European and republican ideals that would go on to forge French history in a federal Europe. Napoleon himself conceded that "There are but two powers in the world, the sword and the mind. In the long run the sword is always beaten by the mind".

C. Peicuti, *The European Economy in 100 Quotes*, Contributions to Economics,
https://doi.org/10.1007/978-3-031-68819-5_5

The fact that at the Congress of Vienna in 1814 and 1815, Talleyrand managed to convince the victorious European nations that France should largely be spared despite having lost the war was beneficial to the construction of Europe. By contrast, the Treaty of Versailles in 1919 imposed a heavy burden on the vanquished nations, which would lead to another world war that undermined European construction.

Europe as an economic entity has since risen from the ashes through the European Union, driven by the tandem formed by France and Germany, with the benediction of Winston Churchill [1874–1965] who, in a speech given on 16 September 1946, declared: "I am now going to say something that will astonish you. The first step in the re-creation of the European family must be a partnership between France and Germany. In this way only can France recover the moral and cultural leadership of Europe. There can be no revival of Europe without a spiritually great France and a spiritually great Germany".[1]

His speech ended with a vision of a new Europe, based on France and Germany working in tandem to defend the right to life and prosperity: "The salvation of the common people of every race and every land from war and servitude must be established on solid foundations, and must be created by the readiness of all men and women to die rather than to submit to tyranny. In this urgent work France and Germany must take the lead together".[2]

As for Charles de Gaulle [1890–1970], he considered that: "In moving toward European unity, we are moving with history".[3]

Money

In his book *Tractatus de Origine, Natura Jure, et Mutacionibus Monetarum*[4] published in 1355, Nicolas Oresme [1320–1382] considered that money did not belong to the Prince and that: "Since money belongs to the community [. . .] it would seem that the community may control it as it wills, and therefore may make as much profit from alteration as it likes, and treat money as its own property". About why the Prince should not debase the coinage, he said: "I am of the opinion that the main and final cause why the Prince pretends to the power of altering the coinage is the profit

[1] Churchill, Winston (1946), Speech delivered at the University of Zurich, 19 September 1946. https://rm.coe.int/16806981f3

[2] Churchill, Winston (1946), Speech delivered at the University of Zurich, 19 September 1946. https://rm.coe.int/16806981f3

[3] Gaulle, Charles de, *Discours et Messages*, Volume II, *Dans l'attente 1946–1958*, Plon, p.466.

[4] *A Treatise on the Origin, Nature Law and Alterations of Money,* translated into French and published under the title *Traictie de la Première Invention des Monnoies.*

or gain which he can get from it." His view was that instead the Prince must "make good œconomy".[5]

In *Le nouveau Cynée,*[6] French political writer Émeric Crucé [1590–1648] was the first to write about the benefits for trade of all European countries adopting a common unit of currency: "It is necessary that Princes of a common consent reduce the moneys to one similar standard, so that each person may make a contract everywhere without damage".[7]

In *Mes pensées,*[8] compiled between 1720 and 1755, the French man of letters, historian, and political philosopher Montesquieu [1689–1755] was the first to mention European humanist patriotism, which in fact appeared much earlier, with the fall of Constantinople in 1453, the year that also marked the end of the 100 Years' War. For many Europeans, there was the realisation that, without this war, Constantinople could have been saved. Montesquieu wrote: "If I knew something that was useful to me and harmful to my family, I would banish it from my mind. If I knew something useful to my family but not to my Country, I would seek to forget it. If I knew something useful to my Country and harmful to Europe, or else useful to Europe and harmful to the human race, I would regard it as a crime".[9]

Central Bank

The Banque de France was created on 18 January 1800. The decree, extracted from the registers of deliberations of the Consuls of the Republic, Paris, 28 Nivôse, Year VIII of the Republic reads:

> The Bank's operations will consist of the discounting of bills of exchange and promissory notes [...] and the issuance of notes payable to the bearer on demand. [...]
>
> These notes will be issued in such proportions that, on account of the cash held by the Bank, and given the maturities of the paper in its portfolio, it will not at any time have exposure such as to require it to defer payment of its commitments.

France would subsequently begin the transition from metallic money to fiduciary money, with the aim of combating inflation. This time, the operation was a success.

---

[5] Oresme, Nicholas, *The De Moneta of Nicholas Oresme and English Mint Documents*, translated from the Latin with Introduction and Notes by Charles Johnson, Thomas Nelson and Sons Ltd., https://cdn.mises.org/The%20De%20Moneta%20of%20Nicholas%20Oresme%20and%20English%20Mint%20Documents_2.pdf

[6] *The New Cyneas.*

[7] Crucé, Émeric (1623), *Le nouveau Cynée,* English from *The New Cyneas*, translated by Boch, Thomas Willing (1929), Allen Lane and Scott.

[8] *My Thoughts.*

[9] Montesquieu, Charles de Secondat, baron de (1720–1755), *Mes pensées*, English from *My Thoughts*, translated by Henry C. Clark, Liberty Fund (2012).

Mind you, this was not the first attempt. In the eighteenth century, France twice tried to set up an institution with the privilege of note issue: Law's Banque Générale, which became the Banque Royale, from 1716 to 1720, and Turgot's Caisse d'escompte, established in 1776. The collapse of Banque Royale as a result of excessive note issuance and speculation had such repercussions that it took two generations before public distrust diminished sufficiently to make it possible to establish a new institution.

Issac Panchaud [London 1737–Auteuil 14 July 1789] convinced Turgot that France needed to emulate Britain and create a central bank modelled on the Bank of England in order to benefit from the same financial solidity. Panchaud made the point that: "Money is the lifeblood of the economy". The Caisse d'escompte was founded in 1776. However, the exponential rise in France's debt put it in difficulty. In 1787, a decision by the King's Council increased its capital to 100 million livres, of which 70 million livres were to be lent to the Treasury. At the same time, in addition to the commercial paper it had discounted, its portfolio consisted of a growing proportion of treasury bills. At the end of 1789, the Constituent Assembly had assignats issued by the Caisse de l'Extraordinaire and prohibited the Caisse d'escompte from issuing any new notes, forcing it to wind down gradually. It was abolished by decree on 24 August 1793.

Jean-Frédéric Perregaux [1744–1808], a banker and shareholder of Caisse d'escompte, convinced the Directoire to establish the Caisse des comptes courants. Later, he proposed to the then First Consul, Napoleon Bonaparte, to transform it into a central bank modelled on the Bank of England. This led to the creation of Banque de France, whose success led to Jean-Frédéric Perregaux being laid to rest at the Pantheon, where France's greats are entombed or commemorated.

Jean-Baptiste Say [1767–1832] considered that money is neutral in the functioning of the economy: "For, after all, money is but the agent of the transfer of values". For him, money performed but a momentary function in the double exchange, which can be conducted more efficiently than through bartering: "For what, in point of fact, do you want the money? Is it not for the purchase of raw materials or stock for your trade, or victuals for your support?"

Euro

In 1855, Victor Hugo [1802–1885] made an impassioned call for a "United States of Europe" and a "continental currency, resting on all Europe as its capital and driven by the activity of two hundred million men. This single currency would replace and bring down all the absurd varieties of money that exist today, with their effigies of princes, those symbols of misery, all being so many causes of impoverishment".

Jacques Rueff [1896–1978], who has a good claim to being France's most distinguished twentieth-century economist, was convinced that: "Europe will be created by means of a single currency or not at all".

Sustainable Development

Antoine de Saint-Exupéry [1900–1944] has these words, lest we forget: "We do not inherit the earth from our parents, we borrow it from our children".[10]

Work

In *Candide*, which was published in 1759, Voltaire [1694–1778] wrote: "Labour keeps off from us three great evils – idleness, vice, and want".[11]

Economic Predictions

Francis I [1494–1547] considered that: "Paris is not a city; it's a country". And that is what it would become increasingly.

In 1863, when he was 35 years, Jules Verne wrote *Paris au XXe siècle*.[12] He described a city crisscrossed by hydrogen-powered buses, cars, and "glittering trains, which seemed to furrow the air with fantastic speed".[13]

"These various improvements were certainly suited to this feverish century, during which the pressure of business permitted no rest or delay. [...] No doubt he would have been astonished; but the men of 1960 were no longer lost in admiration of such marvels; they exploited them quite calmly, without being any the happier, for, from their hurried gait, their peremptory manner, their American "dash," it was apparent that the demon of wealth impelled them onward without mercy or relief".[14]

---

[10] Saint-Exupéry, Antoine de (1939), *Terre des hommes*, Editions Gallimard.

[11] Voltaire (1759, *Candide*, Electronic Scholarly Publishing Project, http://www.esp.org/books/voltaire/candide.pdf

[12] *Paris in the twentieth century.*

[13] Verne, Jules, translated by Howard, Richard (2002), *Paris in the Twentieth Century: The Lost Novel*, Del Rey.

[14] Verne, Jules, translated by Howard, Richard (2002), *Paris in the Twentieth Century: The Lost Novel*, Del Rey.

Jules Verne anticipated the development of the Internet and the financialisation of the economy:

> "But who dreams of being entertained? Let's bore one another to death! That's our ruling principle today!"
> "And you can't see any remedy for it?" Michel asked.
> "None, so long as finance and machinery prevail! And it's really machinery that's doing the mischief".[15]

Jules Verne describes the concentration of the economy and population in modern megacities, envisioning a Greater Paris with its five million inhabitants: "The delimitation of the present capital was marked by the forts of Mont Valérien, Saint-Denis, Aubervilliers, Romainville, Vincennes, Charenton, Vitry, Bicêtre, Montrouge, Vanves, and Issy; [...] It had devoured the entire Department of the Seine".[16]

The book depicted a Parisian society where "if no one read any longer, at least everyone could read, could even write".[17] French has been relegated to the rank of an "ancient language", much like Latin and Greek that "were not only dead languages but buried as well",[18] and at a prize-giving at the most prestigious academic institution of Paris and the country "a Chinese speech replaced [French] to great advantage".[19]

In the book, "the civil service developed in every possible way, shape, and form",[20] the main character bemoans that "there are ten million of them in France; figure the chances of advancement, and take your place in line!"[21]

According to the French National Office for Statistics INSEE, at the end of 2019, 5.66 million persons, or one in five employed persons, worked in the French civil service,[22] compared with one in nine in Germany. Admittedly, this is far less than predicted by Jules Verne, but he was right in his prediction that "government jobs" would multiply; and they still are. In France, the number of civil servants increased by 36.3% between 1980 and 2007, by comparison with which the number of employed persons increased by 16.4% over the same period. In other countries, it was the exact opposite, notably in Germany.

---

[15] Ibid.
[16] Ibid.
[17] Ibid.
[18] Ibid.
[19] Ibid.
[20] Ibid.
[21] Ibid.
[22] https://www.insee.fr/fr/statistiques/5232488#titre-bloc-13

Wealth

Jean Bodin [1529–1596] considered that: "There is no wealth or strength except in men".

In *Béatrix*,[23] which was published in 1839, Honoré de Balzac [1799–1850] observed: "When avarice has an object it ceases to be a vice; it becomes a means of virtue".[24]

François Quesnay [1694–1774] was one of the first to call himself an economist, though he was a doctor of medicine and served as a physician in ordinary to King Louis XV. He defined the wealth of a nation, at a time when agriculture was the main economic activity, as: "Poor peasants; poor kingdom; poor kingdom, poor king".

In *Lettres philosophiques*[25] published in 1734, Voltaire observed: "Many ages passed away before justice could be done to human nature – before mankind were conscious that it was abominable for many to sow, and but few reap".[26]

He also wrote: "In good policy, we have discovered the secret whereby to starve the very people who, by cultivating the land, keep the others alive".[27]

Poverty

In *Voyage au bout de la nuit*[28] published in 1932, Louis-Ferdinand Céline [1894–1961] wrote: "Nearly all a poor bastard's desires are punishable by jail".[29]

In Émile Zola's *L'Assommoir*[30] published in 1877, one of the characters, Gervaise, recalled her ideal life in poverty: "My desire would be to work in peace,

---

[23] *Beatrix.*

[24] Balzac, Honoré de, Beatrix, translated by Katharine Prescott Wormeley, https://www.gutenberg.org/cache/epub/1957/pg1957-images.html

[25] *Letters on the English.*

[26] Voltaire (1734), *Letters on the English*, Blackmask Online, http://public-library.uk/ebooks/58/98.pdf

[27] Le Duc Leouzon, Louis Antoine, *Le Sottisier De Voltaire* (1880), Kessigner Publication.

[28] *Journey to the End of the Night.*

[29] Céline, Louis-Ferdinand (1932), *Journey to the End of the Night*, translated from the French by Ralph Manheim, https://neoalchemist.files.wordpress.com/2012/06/louis-ferdinand-celine-journey-to-the-end-of-the-night.pdf

[30] *The Dram Shop.*

always to have bread to eat, and a decent place to sleep in, you know; just a bed, a table, and two chairs, nothing more".[31]

Arguably, the greatest politician and diplomat in French modern history, Charles Maurice de Talleyrand-Périgord [1754–1838] served as the Foreign Minister under Napoleon I and then Louis XVIII, and was France's chief negotiator at the Congress of Vienna. As Talleyrand explained in his memoirs, "the ranks of the discontented are made up of the thinking poor".[32]

Esther Duflo [1972–] was the first French woman to be awarded a Nobel Prize in Economic Sciences, rewarding her experimental approach to alleviating global poverty. The 2019 Nobel laureate wrote: "When economic development reduces poverty, the condition of women improves on two counts: first, when poverty is reduced, the condition of everyone, including women, improves, and second, gender inequality declines as poverty declines, so the condition of women improves more than that of men with development".[33]

Adding: "Neither economic development nor women's empowerment is the magic bullet it is sometimes made out to be. Equity between men and women is only likely to be achieved by continuing policy actions that favor women at the expense of men, possibly for a very long time".[34]

Taxation

Jean-Baptiste Colbert [1669–1683], who served as Controller-General of Finances for 18 years, stated: "The art of taxation consists in so plucking the goose as to obtain the largest possible amount of feathers with the smallest possible amount of hissing".

The figurehead of Ecole Supérieure de Commerce de Paris (ESCP) Business School, Jean-Baptiste Say, in *Traité d'économie politique*[35] published in 1803, wrote: "Since taxation does, in point of fact, deprive the tax-payer of a product,

[31] Zola, Émile (1915), *The Dram Shop*, edited by Ernest A. Vizetelly, The Marion Company.

[32] Talleyrand-Périgord, Charles-Maurice de (2020), *Charles-Maurice de Talleyrand: mots, propos, aphorismes. Le bréviaire de Talleyrand*, Albin Michel.

[33] Duflo, Esther (2012), *Women Empowerment and Economic Development*, Journal of Economic Literature 2012, 50(4), 1051–1079 https://doi.org/10.1257/jel.50.4.1051

[34] http://www.theatlantic.com/sexes/archive/2012/12/the-challenge-of-closing-the-gender-gap-in-developing-countries/266617/

[35] *A Treatise on Political Economy*.

which is to him, either a means of personal gratification, or a means of reproduction, the lighter the tax is, the less must be the privation".[36]

After studying at the Ecole Supérieure de Commerce de Paris (ESCP) Business School, Joseph Garnier [1813–1881] would hold the positions of assistant professor and then director of studies. He was also a founding member of the Société d'Économie Politique in 1842. A prolific author, he contributed to the *Dictionnaire de l'économie politique* edited by Charles Coquelin and Gilbert-Urbain Guillaumin. One article that appeared in the 1852 edition is devoted to fiscality, explaining how the Latin word fiscus has passed into modern language. In Latin fiscus referred to a moneybag, purse, or basket in which money was kept. In late Latin, it meant of or pertaining to the state treasury. Much as in the French "agir avec fiscalité", fiscality refers to excessive regard for financial considerations, Joseph Garnier explaining that the tax authorities considered taxpayers as adversaries, who could be taxed and exploited at will.

In his *Projet d'une dixme royale*, the famous siege engineer Sébastien Le Prestre, Marquis de Vauban [1633–1707], warned that: "Too many taxes do not increase the product of taxation", in other words too much tax kills tax.

The French writer and humourist Alphonse Allais [1854–1905] estimated that: "Taxes should be asked to do more, the taxpayer less".

Supply

In *Traité d'économie politique*,[37] Jean-Baptiste Say wrote: "Supply creates its own demand"; explaining that: "The success of one branch of commerce supplies more ample means of purchase, and consequently opens a market for the products of all the other branches"; and that: "It is quite impossible that the purchase of one product can be affected, otherwise than by the value of another." And adding that: "But it may be asked, if this be so, how does it happen, that there is at times so great a glut of commodities in the market, and so much difficulty in finding a vent for them? Why cannot one of these superabundant commodities be exchanged for another? I answer that the glut of a particular commodity arises from its having outrun the total demand for it in one or two ways; either because it has been produced in excessive abundance, or because the production of other commodities has fallen short".

[36] Say, Jean Baptiste, *A Treatise on Political Economy, or The Production, Distribution, and Consumption of Wealth*, translated from the fourth edition of the French, by C. R. Prinsep, M.A., Batoche Books.
https://socialsciences.mcmaster.ca/econ/ugcm/3ll3/say/treatise.pdf

[37] *A Treatise on Political Economy.*

And went on to write: "It is because the production of some commodities has declined, that other commodities are superabundant. To use a more hackneyed phrase, people have bought less, because they have made less profit; and they have made less profit for one or two causes; either they have found difficulties in the employment of their productive means, or these means have themselves been deficient".[38]

Finance

For Talleyrand: "Financiers flourish only when nations decline".[39] Also: "If you don't have the means to fulfil your ambitions, you have every right to worry", and: "There is no shortage of dupes but of charlatans".

In the novel *L'Argent*[40] published in 1892, Aristide Saccard, the fictional character created by Émile Zola [1840–1902], starts up a financial establishment, Banque Universelle. This is a hugely successful venture initially: "Money [...] flows like quicksilver and seeps into every crack", with finance irrigating the economy. However, because of insider dealings and manipulations, the bank becomes toxic and fails, and customers lose everything. Nevertheless, in the book's final chapter, Zola's parting words are: "Money was the fertilizer in which tomorrow's humanity would grow, Money was both a poison and a destructive force, but it was also the stimulant necessary to all social growth, a breeding ground for the great works that facilitated life on earth".[41]

Stock Exchange

In *L'Argent,*[42] Zola describes the fever of the markets, specifically the stock market, which in 1891, when he published this novel, had not yet been dematerialised: "He lingered for a moment on the kerb, trembling. It was rush hour, when life in Paris seemed to congregate on this central square, between Rues Montmartre and Richelieu, the two clogged arteries that conveyed the crowds. Carriages flowed non-stop

---

[38] Say, Jean Baptiste, *A Treatise on Political Economy, or The Production, Distribution, and Consumption of Wealth*, translated from the fourth edition of the French, by C. R. Prinsep, M.A., Batoche Books.
https://socialsciences.mcmaster.ca/econ/ugcm/3ll3/say/treatise.pdf

[39] Bernard, J. F. (1973), *Talleyrand: A Biography*, Putnam.

[40] *Money.*

[41] Zola, Emile (2016), *Money*, translated by André Naffis-Sahely, Alma Books.
https://archive.org/details/money0000zola/page/14/mode/2up?q=stream

[42] *Money.*

from the four crossroads at the four points of the square, going up and down the streets amid the agitated crowd of pedestrians".[43]

Talking about the incessant flow of carriages and the throng of people: "From the station, two rows of carriages ran relentlessly alongside the railings, breaking up and then forming again; meanwhile on Rue Vivienne, the Victoria cabs of the introducing brokers stretched out in a tight row, dominated by the coachmen, who, reins in hand, were ready to flog their beasts and whisk off at the first sign. The steps and peristyle of the Exchange were turned black by a swarm of black frock coats; on the kerb market, having already taken their place under the clock, the brokers began their open outcry, the noisy tide of earned interest, overpowering the roar of the city".[44]

And the fascination in which the Stock Exchange was held: "Passers-by turned their heads, both curious and afraid of what was going on in there, those mysterious financial transactions that few French brains could grasp, all those sudden riches and bankruptcies which they could not explain, amid all those hand gestures and savage screams. Deafened by the distant voices and standing at the edge of the stream, being brushed by the throng of people, Saccard began to dream once more of the kingdom of gold in this feverish neighbourhood in the middle of which, from one to three o'clock, the Exchange beat like an enormous heart".[45]

The Palais Brongniart was built at Napoleon's instigation. When he laid the foundation stone in 1808, the Emperor wanted to bring together all stock market activities in one place in order to optimise the existing system. It was the high temple of finance from 1826 to 1998. Until 15 July 1987, the market operated as an open outcry exchange. The move to centralise stock exchanges, which Napoleon saw as a necessity in France, continued throughout the world.

In 1967, Charles de Gaulle declared: "France's policy is not determined on the trading floor".

Automation

Charles Gide [1847–1932], the uncle of the author André Gide, was a professor of political economy at the Collège de France, a prestigious higher education and research establishment. He was involved in rolling out the teaching of economics

[43] Zola, Emile (2016), *Money*, translated by André Naffis-Sahely, Alma Books, https://archive.org/details/money0000zola/page/14/mode/2up?q=stream

[44] Ibid.

[45] Ibid.

at university faculties from 1877, with teaching diplomas starting to be awarded in the field of economic sciences in 1896.

The historic leader of the French cooperative movement, he was one of the founders of Banques Populaires. He became the theorist of what became known as the *École de Nîmes*, a think-tank that studied solidarity pragmatically, as a set of scientifically observable facts essential to the proper functioning of societies and the economy. His work has remained the main reference in social economics to this day.

Charles Gide considered that automation had benefited the economy: "Thanks to the multiplication of books since the invention of printing, there are many more printers to-day than there were copyists in the Middle Ages. Thanks to the railways, there are many more travellers, and therefore many more workmen employed in transport than there were postilions, ostlers, and postmasters. Thanks to mechanical looms, there are many more workers employed in textile industries than there were hand-loom weavers in former days".[46]

He concluded: "In short, the classical argument comes to this: that though the invention of machinery may provoke crises and produce suffering, these are only temporary and right themselves spontaneously".[47]

In *Croissance zéro?*[48] Alfred Sauvy [1898–1990], summarised the writings of Charles Gide in one sentence: "In every country and at every period, without exception, the number of jobs has increased as a result of the machine, contrary to the reputation it has acquired as 'destroyer of jobs'".[49]

In *Philosophie de la misère*[50] published in 1846, Pierre-Joseph Proudhon [1809–1865] delivered the following analysis: "Machines promised us an increase of wealth; they have kept their word, but at the same time endowing us with an increase of poverty. They promised us liberty; I am going to prove that they have brought us slavery".[51]

The economist Jean Fourastié [1907–1990] considered that: "The machine constraints man to specialise in the human".

[46] Gide, Charles (1924), *Principle of Political Economy*, translated by Ernest Row.

[47] Ibid.

[48] *Zero growth?*

[49] Sauvy, Alfred (1976), *Zero growth?*, Praeger.

[50] *The Philosophy of Poverty.*

[51] Proudhon, Pierre-Joseph (1847), The Philosophy of Poverty, by Benjamin R. Tucker (1888), https://www.marxists.org/reference/subject/economics/proudhon/philosophy/

Competition

In *De l'esprit des lois*[52] published in 1748, Montesquieu wrote: "It is competition which sets a just value on merchandises, and establishes the relation between them".[53]

Alexis de Tocqueville [1805–1859] questioned state interventionism in the name of public interest: "The government having stepped into the place of Divine Providence in France, it was but natural that everyone, when in difficulties, invoked its aid. We find vast number of petitions which, though the writers professed to be speaking on behalf of the public, were in reality intended to further their small private interests".[54]

Tocqueville thus takes up the torch from the merchant Le Gendre who, when asked by Colbert "What should we do to help you?" is said to have answered, "Let us be!"

The economist Léon Walras [1834–1910] considered that: "It is positive that political and social economy should be considered a science by certain economists that can be captured in its entirety with four words: Laisser faire, laisser passer".[55] He added, however, that: "To talk of free competition [...] is not say a total absence of state intervention. To begin with, such an intervention is necessary to establish and maintain free competition where it is possible".[56]

In *Harmonies Économiques*,[57] the economist Frédéric Bastiat [1801–1850] explained: "It is obvious that competition is another word for freedom. If you destroy the freedom to act, you destroy the possibility and consequently the right to choose, judge, and compare; you kill the mind, you kill thought, and you kill man himself".[58]

In *Traité et pratique d'économie politique*[59] published in 1896, the economist Paul Leroy-Beaulieu [1843–1916], who was the co-president of *Société d'économie politique*, a French learned society concerned with political economy, wrote:

---

[52] *Spirit Of Laws.*

[53] Montesquieu, Charles de Secondat, baron de (1748), *De l'esprit des lois*, English from *Spirit Of Laws*, translated by Nugent, Thomas, Collingwood (1823).

[54] Tocqueville, Alexis de (1856), *L'Ancien Régime et la Révolution*, English from *The ancien regime and the French Revolution,* translate by Gilbert, Stuart, Collins/Fontana.

[55] Léon Walras, *L'État et le chemin de fer*, 1875.

[56] Léon Walras, *Esquisse d'une doctrine économique et sociale*, 1898.

[57] *Economic Harmonies.*

[58] Bastiat, Frédéric (1851), Economic Harmonies, Liberty Fund Network, https://oll.libertyfund.org/page/cw5

[59] *Treaty and Practice of Political Economy.*

"Competition is the great force, the main force in the economic world. It is at the same time the implosive, regulating and coordinating force par excellence. Without it, there is only chaos, arbitrariness, fantasy and uncertainty".

Private Debt

The debate over the necessity to contract debts and unnecessary expenditure appeared very early in French literature with François Rabelais [1483–1553], the author of the *Tiers Livre*[60] published in 1546.

In Chapters III and IV, Panurge, whom Pantagruel reproaches for eating all the wheat on the ear, praises debt. Panurge has been made squire of the prosperous territory of Salmigondin, but in just 2 weeks has squandered all the money on feasts and banquets. He then borrowed an amount equivalent to the income generated by the estate over 3 years. Pantagruel is opposed to debt, believing that it is laziness that leads people to borrow instead of working for a living. There follows an exchange between the two characters:

> "But, quoth Pantagruel, when will you be out of debt?
>
> At the next ensuing term of the Greek kalends, answered Panurge, when all the world shall be content, and that it be your fate to become your own heir. The Lord forbid that I should be out of debt, as if, indeed, I could not be trusted. Who leaves not some leaven over night, will hardly have paste the next morning. Be still indebted to somebody or other, that there may be somebody always to pray for you, that the giver of all good things may grant unto you a blessed, long, and prosperous life; fearing, if fortune should deal crossly with you, that it might be his chance to come short of being paid by you, he will always speak good of you in every company, ever and anon purchase new creditors unto you [...].And yet did I, in this only respect and consideration of being a debtor, esteem myself worshipful, reverend, and formidable".[61]
>
> To which Panurge replies by praising creditors:
>
> "Nay, creditors, I will maintain it, even to the very fire itself exclusively, are fair and goodly creatures. Who lendeth nothing is an ugly and wicked creature, and an accursed imp of the infernal Old Nick. And there is made—what? Debts. A thing most precious and dainty, of great use and antiquity. [...]Yet doth it not lie in the power of everyone to be a debtor. To acquire creditors is not at the disposure of each man's arbitrament. You nevertheless would deprive me of this sublime felicity. You ask me when I will be out of debt".[62]
>
> For Panurge, debts create bonds that cement society and the universe:
>
> "Well, to go yet further on, and possibly worse in your conceit, may Saint Bablin, the good saint, snatch me, if I have not all my lifetime held debt to be as a union or conjunction of the heavens with the earth, and the whole cement whereby the race of mankind is kept together; yea, of such virtue and efficacy that, I say, the whole progeny of Adam would very

---

[60] *Third Book.*

[61] Rabelais, François (1546), *Gargantua and his Son Pantagruel*, from Urquhart's translation of Book III., which appeared posthumously in 1693, with a new edition of Books I. and II., under Motteux's editorship.

[62] Ibid.

suddenly perish without it. [...] Wherein it is to be supposed there is no debtor or creditor, that is to say, a world without debts. There amongst the planets will be no regular course, all will be in disorder".[63]

His view is that: "Venus will be no more venerable, because she shall have lent nothing. The moon will remain bloody and obscure. For to what end should the sun impart unto her any of his light? He owed her nothing. Nor yet will the sun shine upon the earth, nor the stars send down any good influence. [...] There would likewise be in such a world no manner of symbolization, alteration, nor transmutation amongst the elements; for the one will not esteem itself obliged to the other, as having borrowed nothing at all from it. Earth then will not become water, water will not be changed into air, of air will be made no fire, and fire will afford no heat unto the earth".[64]

Without debts, "The earth will produce nothing but monsters, Titans, giants; no rain will descend upon it, nor light shine thereon; no wind will blow there, nor will there be in it any summer or harvest. Lucifer will break loose, and issuing forth of the depth of hell, accompanied with his furies, fiends, and horned devils, will go about to unnestle and drive out of heaven all the gods, as well of the greater as of the lesser nations. Such a world without lending will be no better than a dog-kennel [...]".[65]

Without debt, men will not come to each other's help: "Men will not then salute one another; it will be but lost labour to expect aid or succour from any, or to cry fire, water, murder, for none will put to their helping hand. Why? He lent no money, there is nothing due to him. Nobody is concerned in his burning, in his shipwreck, in his ruin, or in his death; and that because he hitherto had lent nothing, and would never thereafter have lent anything. In short, Faith, Hope, and Charity would be quite banished from such a world—for men are born to relieve and assist one another; and in their stead should succeed and be introduced Defiance, Disdain, and Rancour, with the most execrable troop of all evils, all imprecations, and all miseries".[66]

Without debts, the world will undergo a metamorphosis: "Whereupon you will think, and that not amiss, that Pandora had there spilt her unlucky bottle. Men unto men will be wolves, hobthrushers, and goblins (as were Lycaon, Bellerophon, Nebuchodonosor), plunderers, highway robbers, cutthroats, rapparees, murderers, poisoners, assassinators, lewd, wicked, malevolent, pernicious haters, set against everybody, like to Ishmael, Metabus, or Timon the Athenian, who for that cause was named Misanthropos, in such sort that it would prove much more easy in nature to have fish entertained in the air and bullocks fed in the bottom of the ocean, than to support or tolerate a rascally rabble of people that will not lend. These fellows, I vow, do I hate with a perfect hatred".[67]

And the body will no longer obey: "And if, conform to the pattern of this grievous, peevish, and perverse world which lendeth nothing, you figure and liken the little world, which is man, you will find in him a terrible justling coil and clutter. The head will not lend the sight of his eyes to guide the feet and hands; the legs will refuse to bear up the body; the hands will leave off working any more for the rest of the members; the heart will be weary of its continual motion for the beating of the pulse, and will no longer lend his assistance; the lungs will withdraw the use of their bellows; the liver will desist from convoying any more blood through the veins for the good of the whole; he bladder will not be indebted to the kidneys, so that the urine thereby will be totally stopped. The brains, in the interim,

---

[63] Ibid.

[64] Ibid.

[65] Rabelais, François (1546), *Gargantua and his Son Pantagruel*, from Urquhart's translation of Book III., which appeared posthumously in 1693, with a new edition of Books I. and II., under Motteux's editorship.

[66] Ibid.

[67] Ibid.

considering this unnatural course, will fall into a raving dotage, and withhold all feeling from the sinews and motion from the muscles".[68]

Leading to death: "Briefly, in such a world without order and array, owing nothing, lending nothing, and borrowing nothing, you would see a more dangerous conspiration than that which Aesop exposed in his Apologue. Such a world will perish undoubtedly; and not only perish, but perish very quickly. Were it Aesculapius himself, his body would immediately rot, and the chafing soul, full of indignation, take its flight to all the devils of hell after my money".[69]

Panurge contrasts this with an ideal world: "On the contrary, be pleased to represent unto your fancy another world, wherein everyone lendeth and everyone oweth, all are debtors and all creditors. O how great will that harmony be, which shall thereby result from the regular motions of the heavens! Methinks I hear it every whit as well as ever Plato did. What sympathy will there be amongst the elements! O how delectable then unto nature will be our own works and productions! Whilst Ceres appeareth laden with corn, Bacchus with wines, Flora with flowers, Pomona with fruits, and Juno fair in a clear air, wholesome and pleasant. I lose myself in this high contemplation".[70]

That is close to paradise: "Then will among the race of mankind peace, love, benevolence, fidelity, tranquillity, rest, banquets, feastings, joy, gladness, gold, silver, single money, chains, rings, with other ware and chaffer of that nature be found to trot from hand to hand. No suits at law, no wars, no strife, debate, nor wrangling; none will be there a usurer, none will be there a pinch-penny, a scrape-good wretch, or churlish hard-hearted refuser. Good God! Will not this be the golden age in the reign of Saturn? The true idea of the Olympic regions, wherein all (other) virtues cease, charity alone ruleth, governeth, domineereth, and triumpheth? All will be fair and goodly people there, all just and virtuous. O happy world! O people of that world most happy! Yea, thrice and four times blessed is that people!"[71]

As pointed out by Céline: "You don't die of debts. You die from not being able to take on debts".

Interest Rates

In *De l'esprit des lois*[72] published in 1748, Montesquieu wrote: "In order that trade may be successfully carried on, it is necessary that a price be fixed on the use of specie; but this should be very inconsiderable. If it be too high, the merchant who sees that it will cost him more in interest than he can gain by commerce will

[68] Ibid.

[69] Ibid.

[70] Rabelais, François (1546), *Gargantua and his Son Pantagruel*, from Urquhart's translation of Book III., which appeared posthumously in 1693, with a new edition of Books I. and II., under Motteux's editorship.

[71] Ibid.

[72] *Spirit Of Laws.*

undertake nothing; if there is no consideration to be paid for the use of specie, nobody will lend it; and here too the merchant will undertake nothing".[73]

In *Réflexions sur la formation et la distribution des richesses*[74] published in 1766, Anne Robert Jacques Turgot [1727–1781] explained that: "The rate of interest is by no means founded [...] on the profit the borrower hopes to make, with the capital of which he purchases the use. This rate like the price of all other merchandise, is fixed by the circumstances of buyer and seller; by the proportion of the sum offered with the demand".[75]

And he goes on: "It is not therefore the quantity of silver [...] which causes the rate of interest to rise or fall, or which brings more money in the market to be lent [...]. It is the accumulated savings which are offered to the borrowers, and the more there are of them, the lower the interest of money will be, at least if the number of borrowers is not augmented in proportion".[76]

Public Debt

Anne-Robert-Jacques Baron de Turgot, after his appointment as Controller-General of Finance, wrote to Louis XVI, then twenty and who had been on the throne for just a few months, to proffer advice: "In the present moment, I confine myself, Sire, to call to your recollection three ideas:

> No national bankruptcy.
> No increase in taxes.
> No new loans.
> No bankruptcy - neither avowed nor disguised under compulsory reductions.
> No increase of taxes—the reasons for this measure Your Majesty will find in the situation of your people, and still more in your own heart.
>
> No new loans - for every loan, by diminishing the amount of the free revenue, necessarily produces at last a bankruptcy, or an increase of taxes. In a period of peace, money should not be borrowed, unless to liquidate old debts, or to discharge others bearing a higher interest.
> To obtain these three points there is but one method, that of reducing the expenditure below the receipt, and so much below it as to leave twenty millions [livres] every year for the

[73]Montesquieu, Charles de Secondat, baron de (1748), *De l'esprit des lois*, English from *Spirit Of Laws*, translated by Nugent, Thomas, Collingwood (1823).

[74]*Reflections on the Formation and Distribution of Wealth.*

[75]Turgot, Anne-Robert-Jacques Baron de (1776), *Reflections on the Formation and Distribution of Wealth*, https://www.econlib.org/library/Essays/trgRfl.html

[76]Ibid.

redemption of former debts. Without this precaution, the first cannonball that is fired will force the state to a public bankruptcy".[77]

For Jean-Marc Daniel [1954–], a professor at ESCP BS and President of Société d'Économie Politique, there is no "good debt" in the market economy: "While one can talk of a 'good deficit' - cyclical deficit - and a bad deficit - structural deficit - there is no such thing as 'good debt'. Debt is the accumulation of structural deficits since, over the course of a cycle, a cyclical deficit is followed by a cyclical surplus, and they end up cancelling each other out. Only the structural deficit adds to the debt. Leaving the structural deficit to run unchecked leads to an accumulation of debt that ends up stifling public action, threatening the sovereign credit rating, and deterring the markets from financing the cyclical deficit, though this is necessary to stabilise the economy".[78]

In *Le Cercle de famille*[79] published in 1932, André Maurois [1885–1967] wrote: "Governments are as old as their finances, as men are as old as their arteries".[80]

Inflation

Pierre-Paul Le Mercier de La Rivière [1720–1794], a French colonial administrator and physiocrat economist, who wrote *L'ordre naturel et essentiel des sociétés politiques*,[81] defined inflation as follow: "As money multiplies, so it loses its market value".

Establishment

Talleyrand: "In the big courts, there's another way of growing taller: it's by bending over".

Talleyrand: "Be at their feet. At their knees... But never in their hands".

---

[77] Turgot, Anne-Robert-Jacques Baron de (1774), *Letter to the King on Finance*, from Soulavie, Jean-Louis (1802), Historical and Political Memoirs of the Reign of Lewis XVI from His Marriage to His Death, Translated from the French, in Six Volumes, vol. 3, London: G. and J. Robinson.

[78] https://www.lefigaro.fr/economie/le-scan-eco/decryptage/2015/07/01/29002-20150701 ARTFIG00019-jean-marc-daniel-il-n-y-a-pas-de-bonne-dette.php

[79] *The Family Circle.*

[80] Maurois, André (1932), *The Family Circle*, translated by Miles Hamish, D. Appleton.

[81] *The Natural and Essential Order of Political Societies.*

Money

In *Les lettres persanes*[82] published in 1721, Montesquieu had this damming comment: "There is nothing more absurd than to cause countless numbers of men to perish in extracting from the bowels of the earth gold and silver, metals in themselves absolutely useless, and which constitute wealth only because they have been chosen as the symbols of it".[83]

Montesquieu would be delighted to know that modern currencies are not of silver or gold and that modern money is no longer backed by gold. But it has to be said that this ability to issue unlimited amounts of money (no longer limited by the gold held in reserves) creates inflation and speculative bubbles, and allows us to live beyond our means, thereby destabilising the market economy.

As explained by Jean-Baptiste Say in *Traité d'économie politique*[84] published in 1803: "All produce [...] is ultimately converted into other produce [...]. Money is but the agent of the transfer of values".[85]

When 24, Alexandre Dumas *fils* [1824–1895] wrote in the Preface to *La Dame aux camélias*[86]: "Esteem money neither more nor less than it deserves, it is a good servant and a bad master".

Transposed to entrepreneurship, it is a reminder that every business has a social purpose, not a financial one. It must be profitable, but its purpose is not reduced to money.

In *Lettre à Madame d'Épinay*[87] of 26 December 1760, Voltaire [1694–1778] wrote: "When it is a question of money, everybody is of the same religion".

Property developer Yoann Choin-Joubert [1975–] said: "It's the money I don't have that costs the most", as to build anything you have advance funds to buy the land, then to construct the building, and only then can you sell the apartments.

---

[82] *Persian Letters.*

[83] Montesquieu, Charles de Secondat, baron de (1881), *Persian Letters*, translated by Davidson, John, George Routledge & Son.

[84] *A Treatise on Political Economy, or The Production, Distribution, and Consumption of Wealth.*

[85] Say, Jean Baptiste, *A Treatise on Political Economy, or The Production, Distribution, and Consumption of Wealth*, translated from the fourth edition of the French, by C. R. Prinsep, M.A., Batoche Books, https://socialsciences.mcmaster.ca/econ/ugcm/3ll3/say/treatise.pdf

[86] *The Lady of the Camellias.*

[87] *Letter to Madame d'Épinay.*

Economy

Jean-Baptise Say believed that: "True economy is the offspring of prudence and sound reason, and does not sacrifice necessaries to superfluities".

Economic Science

In *Traité d'économie politique*[88] published in 1616, Antoine de Montchrestien provided the following definition: "Political economy is the science of increasing a kingdom's riches".

In *Trattato di sociologia generale*[89] published in 1916, Vilfredo Pareto [1848–1923] wrote: "Until economic science is much farther advanced, 'economic principles' are less important to the economists than the reciprocal bearings of the results of economics and the results of the other social sciences. Many economists are paying no attention to such interrelations, for mastery of them is a long and fatiguing task requiring an extensive knowledge of facts".[90]

International Trade

In *Traité d'économie politique*,[91] Antoine de Montchrestien stated: "Money is needed, and there being none of our doing, it must be obtained from foreigners".

But he also insisted: "Every society must be abundantly supplied, and must not borrow elsewhere what it needs, for, since it necessarily places itself at the mercy of others, it makes itself weak to that extent". Antoine de Montchrestien wrote in 1616 what we discovered three centuries later during the COVID-19 crisis.

Jean-Baptiste Colbert considered that it was necessary to: "Increase money in commerce by attracting money from countries whence it comes, keeping it in the kingdom, by preventing it from leaving, giving men the means to profit from it".

---

[88] *Treatise of Political Economy.*

[89] *The Mind and Society - A Treatise on General Sociology.*

[90] Pareto, Vilfredo (1963), *The Mind and Society - A Treatise on General Sociology*, translated by Andrew Bongiorno and Arthur Livingston with the advice and active cooperation of James Harvey Rogers, edited by Arthur Livingston, Dover Publications Inc., New York.

[91] *Treatise of Political Economy.*

In *De l'esprit des lois,*[92] Montesquieu's view was that: "Commerce is a cure for the most destructive prejudices; for it is almost a general rule, that wherever we find agreeable manners, there commerce flourishes".[93]

He goes on: "Two nations who traffic with each other become reciprocally dependent; for if one has an interest in buying, the other has an interest in selling: and thus their union is founded on their mutual necessities".[94]

Jules Vernes described the happy outcome of globalization thus: "The links of commerce are drawing nations ever closer! The British, the Russians, the Americans all have their banknotes, their rubles, their dollars invested in our commercial enterprises".[95] He describes a country where the British are gradually becoming the great landowners, taking their revenge on William the Conqueror. And he goes on: "For it's the century's profession of faith: with Montaigne and maybe Rabelais it was what do I know? In the nineteenth century it was what does it matter to me? And nowadays we say: how much does it earn? Well, the day a war earns as much as an industrial investment, then there'll be wars".[96]

In *Dictionnaire des idées reçues,*[97] Gustave Flaubert [1821–1880] wrote: "Imports: Canker at the heart of trade".

In *Grandeur et décadence de César Birotteau*[98] published in 1837, Honoré de Balzac observed: "He was meditating on the labels and the shape of the bottles, discussing the quality of the corks, the color of the placards. And yet people say there is no poetry in commerce!"[99]

---

[92] *Spirit Of Laws.*

[93] Montesquieu, Charles de Secondat, baron de (1748), *De l'esprit des lois*, English from *Spirit Of Laws*, translated by Nugent, Thomas, Collingwood (1823).

[94] Ibid.

[95] Verne, Jules, translated by Howard, Richard (2002), *Paris in the Twentieth Century: The Lost Novel*, Del Rey.

[96] Verne, Jules (2002), *Paris in the Twentieth Century: The Lost Novel*, translated by Howard, Richard, Del Rey.

[97] *Dictionary of Received Ideas.*

[98] *Rise and Fall of Cesar Birotteau.*

[99] Balzac, Honoré de (2010), *Rise and Fall of Cesar Birotteau*, translated by Katharine Prescott Wormeley, Project Gutenberg, https://www.gutenberg.org/files/1942/1942-h/1942-h.htm

Technique

In *Discours préliminaire à l'Encyclopédie*[100] published in 1751, Jean Le Rond d'Alembert [1717–1783] stated: "The contempt in which the mechanical arts are held seems to have affected to some degree even their inventors. The names of these benefactors of humankind are almost all unknown, whereas the history of its destroyers, that is to say, of the conquerors, is known to everyone. However, it is perhaps in the artisan that one must seek the most admirable evidences of the sagacity, the patience, and the resources of the mind".[101]

In *Plaidoyer pour l'avenir*[102] published in 1961, Louis François Armand [1905–1971] contended that: "It is not technology that represents the real danger for civilisation, but the inertia of the structures".

In *Oppression et liberté*[103] published in 1955, the philosopher Simone Weil [1909–1943] drew attention to the fact that: "The higher the level of technical efficiency the more the advantages to be derived from new developments diminish as compared with the drawbacks".[104]

Liberalism

Turgot, France's former Controller-General of Finance, wrote: "Thus our policy should surrender itself to the course of nature, and the course of commerce, which is no less necessary and no less irresistible than the course of nature, without seeking to direct this course. For, in order to guide it without disturbing it, and without injuring ourselves, it would be necessary for us to be able to follow all the changes in the needs, the interests, and the industry of mankind. It would be necessary to know these in such detail as would be physically impossible to obtain and in which even the most skilful, the most active and the most painstaking government will risk always to be wrong in half the cases".[105]

[100] Preliminary Discourse to the Encyclopedia of Diderot.

[101] d'Alembert, Jean-Baptiste le Rond (1995), *Preliminary Discourse to the Encyclopedia of Diderot*, translated by Richard N. Schwab with the collaboration of Walter E. Rex, Chicago: University of Chicago Press, 1995).

[102] *Plea for the Future.*

[103] *Oppression and Liberty.*

[104] Simone Weil (1958), *Oppression and Liberty*, translated by Arthur Wills and John Petrie, https://theanarchistlibrary.org/library/simone-weil-oppression-and-liberty

[105] Turgot, Jacques (1773), *Letter to l'Abbé Terray on the "Marque des Fers"*, from the Turgot Collection, edited by David Gordon, Mises Institute.
https://cdn.mises.org/The%20Turgot%20Collection%20Writings,%20Speeches,%20and%20Letters%20of%20Anne%20Robert%20Jacques%20Turgot,%20Baron%20de%20Laune_2.pdf

In 1794, at the age of 39 years, Talleyrand, for cause of the French Revolution, discovered the United States, the land of liberalism. He observed: "There are more ways of making a fortune here than in any other place". Later, he exclaimed: "Don't talk to me about a country where I haven't found anyone who wouldn't sell me their dog". He wrote: "Turning to America, Europe must always keep its eyes open, and provide no pretext for recrimination or reprisals. America is growing by the day. It will become a colossal power, and a time must come when, placed vis-à-vis Europe in easier communication by means of new discoveries, it will wish to have its say in our affairs and involve itself in them".

In 1803, in *Traité d'économie politique*, Jean-Baptiste Say declared: "Perfection in administration is to administer little".

In 1815, in *Catéchisme d'économie politique,*[106] Jean-Baptiste Say wrote: "In matters of State, I prone abstention"; adding: "You are never better governed than when there is no government".

In 1833, in *Le médecin de campagne,*[107] Honoré de Balzac wrote: "The idler's life alone is a costly one, and I am not sure that the unproductive consumer is not robbing the community at large".[108]

The first Frenchman to be awarded the Nobel Prize in Economics in 1983, Gérard Debreu [1921–2004] stated: "The superiority of liberalism has been demonstrated mathematically".

Communism

Victor Hugo explained: "Communism. Equality of eagles and sparrows, humming-birds and bats, all wingspans in the same cage, all gazes staring into the same crepuscule, that's not for me".

Consumption

In *Catéchisme d'économie politique* published in 1815, Jean-Baptiste Say wrote: "What is consumption? It is to destroy the utility of a product, in so doing remove the value conferred by this utility".

---

[106] *Catechism of Political Economy.*

[107] *The Country Doctor.*

[108] Balzac, Honoré de (2010), *The Country Doctor*, translated by Ellen Marriage and Clara Bell, Project Gutenberg, https://www.gutenberg.org/files/1350/1350-h/1350-h.htm

As explained by the fictional character Octave Mouret in Émile Zola's *Au bonheur des dames*[109] published in 1883, for a department store to make profits and swallow up all the small competing stores, it needs a volume strategy: "You sell cheap in order to sell a quantity, and you sell a quantity in order to sell cheap".[110]

Social Ascension

Born to a prosperous middle-class family, Nicolas Fouquet would rise to the position of Superintendent of Finances under Louis XIV. He built Vaux-le-Vicomte, the model for Versailles. He paid a pension to La Fontaine and discovered Molière, Le Nôtre and Lebrun. The motto on his coat of arms, depicting a squirrel (*foucquet* in French), speaks of the man: *Quo non ascendet?* ("What heights will he not scale?").

Talleyrand considered that: "There are two ways to rise, by your talent or the imbecility of others".

His view was that: "High places are like steep rocks, only accessible to eagles and reptiles".

Talleyrand explained that: "Men are like statues, you have to see them in situ".

He observed that: "The elevation of a mediocre man will take him to a high place, from which the world below looks small, and from where he looks small to the world".

According to Talleyrand: "When ten steps are needed and you have taken nine, you are halfway there".

Power

According to Talleyrand: "Power isn't about hitting hard and often, it's about hitting right".

[109] *The Ladies' Paradise.*

[110] Zola, Émile (1883), *The Ladies' Paradise*, translated by Vizetelly, Ernest Alfred (2017), https://www.gutenberg.org/cache/epub/54726/pg54726-images.html

Action

For Talleyrand: "In matters of importance, refrain from asking for advice: it is necessary to weigh, dare and act".

Success

It was Talleyrand's belief that: "Where so many men have failed, a woman can succeed".

According to Talleyrand: "The difficult time is not during the struggle, it comes with success". It is not enough to succeed, you have to capitalise on success and do so quickly.

Savoir-Faire

For Talleyrand: "There is no accident so unfortunate that a skilful man cannot put to good advantage, or one so fortunate that an imprudent man cannot turn to his disadvantage".

He observed: "People who do nothing are convinced they can do everything".

Also: "Be a lion in triumph, a fox in defeat, a snail in counsel, and a bird in action".

According to him: "Skilful, light-weight men float like cork through storms". And: "When all is lost, it's time for great souls".

For Talleyrand: "There are three types of knowledge: knowledge per se, knowing how to behave and knowing how to do; the last two generally dispense with the need for the first".

Teamwork

According to Talleyrand: "The worst wheel of the cart makes the most noise".

He stated: "I am more afraid of an army of one hundred sheep led by a lion than an army of one hundred lions led by a sheep".

Talleyrand observed: "In chess, the bishops [*les fous* in French, the fools] stand nearest to the kings".

He had these words of advice: "You have to lead people without making them feel the yoke, enslave their wills without forcing them".

Timeliness

Talleyrand believed: "Much time is lost from not having time".

He drew attention to the fact that: "A jug of water is all it takes to stop the beginnings of a fire; a moment later, a bucket; later, pumps are needed, by when the house is engulfed in flames".

Confidentiality

According to Talleyrand: "Words held back are your slave; words uttered are your master".

He added: "The fault for betraying a secret lies with the one having entrusted this secret".

Confidence

As Talleyrand observed: "You only believe in those who believe in themselves".

Talleyrand has this to say about Napoleon: "This is a man who believes he is the master of destiny and whose astonishing confidence in his star inspires such an astonishing sense of security in his followers".

Corruption

Talleyrand: "Every time I visited a capital, I was warned that I was in the most corrupt city in Europe, and it was true".

Diminishing Returns

In 1768, in *Observations sur le mémoire de M. De Saint-Péravy,*[111] Turgot explained, before David Ricardo [1772–1823], the concept of diminishing returns: "The earth certainly has a limited fertility, and assuming it to have been ploughed, manured, marled, ditched, watered, weeded, as far as it can be, it is obvious that all further expenditure would be useless, and that such increases could even become detrimental. In this case, the advances would be increased without increasing the product. There is therefore a maximum point of production which it is impossible to pass, and when this point has been reached, advances will not only cease producing 250 for 100, but will produce absolutely nothing.

While it may be granted to the author that, in the case of ordinary good cultivation, the annual advances return 250 for 100, it is more than likely that as the advances are increased gradually past this point up to the point where they return nothing, each increase would be less and less productive".[112]

Value

In *Réflexions sur la formation et la redistribution des richesses,*[113] Turgot considered that: "The value of the thing exchanged has no other measure than the needs or desires of one party weighed with those of the other, and is fixed only by their agreement".[114]

Ownership

In 1803, in *Traité d'économie politique,*[115] Jean-Baptiste Say wrote: "Political economy recognises the right of property solely as the most powerful of all encouragements to the multiplication of wealth".[116]

---

[111] *Observations on a Paper by Saint-Péravey.*

[112] Turgot, Jacques (1768), *Observations on a Paper by Saint-Péravey*, from the Turgot Collection, edited by David Gordon, Mises Institute.
https://cdn.mises.org/The%20Turgot%20Collection%20Writings,%20Speeches,%20and%20Letters%20of%20Anne%20Robert%20Jacques%20Turgot,%20Baron%20de%20Laune_2.pdf

[113] *Reflections on the Formation and Distribution of Wealth.*

[114] Turgot, Jacques (1768), *Reflections on the Formation and Distribution of Wealth*, from the Turgot Collection, edited by David Gordon, Mises Institute.
https://cdn.mises.org/The%20Turgot%20Collection%20Writings,%20Speeches,%20and%20Letters%20of%20Anne%20Robert%20Jacques%20Turgot,%20Baron%20de%20Laune_2.pdf

[115] *A Treatise on Political Economy, or The Production, Distribution, and Consumption of Wealth.*

[116] Say, Jean Baptiste, *A Treatise on Political Economy, or The Production, Distribution, and Consumption of Wealth*, translated from the fourth edition of the French, by C. R. Prinsep, M.A., Batoche Books, https://socialsciences.mcmaster.ca/econ/ugcm/3ll3/say/treatise.pdf

In *Le médecin de campagne*,[117] Honoré de Balzac explained: "No matter how unwholesome his hovel may be, a peasant clings far more to it than a banker does to his mansion. The reason of it? That I do not know. Perhaps thoughts and feelings are strongest in those who have but few of them, simply because they have but few. Perhaps material things count for much in the lives of those who live so little in thought; certain it is that the less they have, the dearer their possessions are to them".[118]

Equality

As put by Charles de Gaulle: "Every Frenchman wants to enjoy one or more privileges; that's his way of showing his passion for equality".

[117] *The Country Doctor.*

[118] Balzac, Honoré de (2010), *The Country Doctor*, translated by Ellen Marriage and Clara Bell, Project Gutenberg, https://www.gutenberg.org/files/1350/1350-h/1350-h.htm

Germany

Activity

Having earlier been appointed to the Privy Council of the Duchy of Weimar, Johann Wolfgang von Goethe [1749–1832] took on the War Commission in 1779, in addition to the Mines and Highways commissions, and in 1782 became Chancellor of the Exchequer. Goethe thus came to be in charge of the duchy's economy, finances, mines, highways, and waterways. Faust, Part II, reflects more particularly the thoughts of Goethe the economist, who besides being acquainted with the theory gained considerable practical experience.

Magical Money

In Faust, Part II, the Devil proposes the creation of paper money to mankind represented by Faust. This paper money is in fact more than a banknote, it is magical money that ultimately refers only to itself and depends only on the infinite trust that men place in it. For Goethe, the creation of magic money *ex nihilo* is a pact with the Devil designed to solve all the cash flow problems of the emperor of the Holy Roman Empire of the German Nation. This creation takes place during a carnival, a celebration of the overthrow of the established order and its replacement by a new order, which magical money would later overthrow in its turn:

> The Steward (Entering hastily.)
> Your Supreme Highness, I never thought
> To announce such luck, the finest wrought,
> As this is, for me the greatest blessing,
> Which I've revealed in your presence:
> For debt after debt I've accounted,

C. Peicuti, *The European Economy in 100 Quotes*, Contributions to Economics,
https://doi.org/10.1007/978-3-031-68819-5_6

The usurer's claws now are blunted,
I'm free of Hell's pain, and then,
It can't be any brighter in Heaven.

The Commander in Chief (Follows hastily.)
Something's paid of what we owe,
The Army's all renewed their vow,
The Cavalry's fresh blood is up,
And girls and landlords can sup.

The Chancellor (Coming forward slowly.)
I'm happy enough to do so, in my old age. –
See and hear the scroll, heavy with destiny,
That's changed to happiness, our misery.
To whom it concerns, may you all know,
This paper's worth a thousand crowns, or so.
As a secure pledge, it will underwrite,
All buried treasure, our Emperor's right.
Now, as soon as the treasure's excavated,
It's taken care of, and well compensated.

The Emperor
I smell a fraud, a monstrous imposture!
Who forged the Emperor's signature?
Have they gone unpunished for their crime?

The Treasurer
Remember! You yourself it was that signed:
Last night. You acted as great Pan
Here's how the Chancellor's speech began:
'Grant yourself this great festive pleasure,
The People's Good: a few strokes of the feather.'
You wrote it here, and while night ruled the land,
A thousand artists created another thousand,
So all might benefit from your good deed,
We stamped the whole series with your screed,
Tens, Thirties, Fifties, Hundreds, all are done.
You can't think how well the folk get on.
See your city once half-dead with decay,
Now all's alive, enjoying its new day!
Though your name's long filled the world with glee,
They've never gazed at it so happily.

The Emperor:
And my people value it as gold, you say?
The Court and Army treat it as real pay?
Then I must yield, though it's wonderful to me.

Mephistopheles issues paper money as counterparty hypothetical riches and treasures hidden in "deep earth", which under Roman law were the Emperor's property. The magical money is in fact based on as-yet-undiscovered treasures:

Faust
'The wealth of treasure that solidifies,
That in your land, in deep earth lies,
Is all unused. In our boldest thought,
Such riches are only feebly caught:
Imagination, in its highest flight,
Strives to, but can't reach that height.'

Magical money benefits from limitless confidence:

Faust
But grasping Spirits, worthy to look deeply,
Trust in things without limit, limitlessly.[1]

It is significant that the emperor should represent the great Pan during the carnival. According to Greek mythology, Pan caused people to lose their minds through the collective panic fright (Greek: *panikon deima*, panikon meaning pertaining to Pan) he inspired. The modern economy is thus placed under the sign of fear. It generates fear, the fear of losing one's job, the fear of not having enough, the fear of not owning everything, the fear that even when surrounded by wealth something is missing. As Faust says: "To feel in the midst of this wealth, what we lack, is to undergo the cruellest of tortures".[2]

Later there would be bank panics...

Modern Times

Goethe saw the dawn of modern times, bringing with it the Industrial Revolution, characterised by incessant activity. In Faust, Part II, Goethe replaced "In the beginning was the verb" by "In the beginning was the act".

In Faust, Part II, Mephistopheles and Faust decide together to put fire to the haven of the old world, which is like a thorn in Faust's side:

Faust
My realm's laid out there, endlessly,
But, at my back, this vexes so,
Proclaiming, with its jealous sound:
My great estate is less than fine,
The old hut, all the trees around,
The crumbling chapel, are not mine.
And even if I wished to rest there,
A strange shadow makes me shudder,
It's a thorn in my eye, and deeper:

[1] https://antilogicalism.com/wp-content/uploads/2017/07/faust.pdf
[2] Ibid.

Oh! Would I were somewhere other!

What used to please my eyes, below,
Has vanished with the centuries.[3]

On the charred remains of his great estate, Faust plans to build a belvedere "to gaze into the infinite".

In Faust, Part II, Goethe describes the destruction of Creation, of what has been bequeathed to us and, subsequently, the emergence of a new world that radically turns its back on Creation. This obsession with the infinite, with the limitless, is the hallmark of our century. In the face of climate change, it is time for us to modify our paradigm and start thinking about our lives and the world differently.

Capitalism

In *Die protestantische Ethik und der Geist des Kapitalismus*[4] published in 1905, Max Weber [1864–1920] defined capitalism as "the most fateful force in modern life". He wrote: "The impulse to acquisition, pursuit of gain, of money, the greatest possible amount of money, has in itself nothing to do with capitalism. [...] Capitalism may even be identical with the restraint, or at least a rational tempering, of this irrational impulse. But capitalism is identical with the pursuit of profit, and forever renewed profit, by means of continuous, rational, capitalistic enterprise. For it must be so: in a wholly capitalistic order of society, an individual capitalistic enterprise which did not take advantage of its opportunities for profit-making would be doomed to extinction".[5]

Max Weber wrote about the spirit of modern capitalism such as it transpires from Benjamin Franklin's autobiography. He considered that there was a type of capitalism specific to Western Europe and the United States: "Capitalism existed in China, India, Babylon, in the classic world, and in the Middle Ages. But in all these cases, as we shall see, this particular ethos was lacking.

Now, all of Franklin's moral attitudes are coloured with utilitarianism. Honesty is useful, because it assures credit; so are punctuality, industry, frugality, and that is the reason they are virtues. A logical deduction from this would be that where, for instance, the appearance of honesty serves the same purpose, that would suffice, and

[3] https://antilogicalism.com/wp-content/uploads/2017/07/faust.pdf

[4] *The Protestant Ethic and the Spirit of Capitalism.*

[5] Weber, Max (1904–1905), *The Protestant Ethic and the Spirit Of Capitalism*, English version translated by Parsons, Talcott (1930), George Allen & Unwin Ltd.

an unnecessary surplus of this virtue would evidently appear to Franklin's eyes as unproductive waste".[6]

And he continued: "And as a matter of fact, the story in his autobiography of his conversion to those virtues, or the discussion of the value of a strict maintenance of the appearance of modesty, the assiduous belittlement of one's own deserts in order to gain general recognition later, confirms this impression. According to Franklin, those virtues, like all others, are only in so far virtues as they are actually useful to the individual, and the surrogate of mere appearance is always sufficient when it accomplishes the end in view. It is a conclusion which is inevitable for strict utilitarianism".[7]

However, he added: "The impression of many Germans that the virtues professed by Americanism are pure hypocrisy seems to have been confirmed by this striking case. But in fact the matter is not by any means so simple. Benjamin Franklin's own character, as it appears in the really unusual candidness of his autobiography, belies that suspicion. The circumstance that he ascribes his recognition of the utility of virtue to a divine revelation which was intended to lead him in the path of righteousness, shows that something more than mere garnishing for purely egocentric motives is involved".[8]

One thing is certain: the virtues evoked by Benjamin Franklin and commented on by Max Weber remain indispensable in business. For this reason, they are often displayed in relations with bankers, for example.

Max Weber further explained: "The religious valuation of restless, continuous, systematic work [...] as the highest means to asceticism [...] must have been the most powerful conceivable lever for the expansion of that attitude toward life which we have here called the spirit of capitalism".[9]

Wealth

Max Weber explained: "When the imagination of a whole people has once been turned toward purely quantitative bigness, as in the United States, this romanticism of numbers exercises an irresistible appeal to the poets among business men".[10]

---

[6]Ibid.
[7]Ibid.
[8]Ibid.
[9]Ibid.
[10]Ibid.

Entrepreneur

In *Die protestantische Ethik und der Geist des Kapitalismus,*[11] Max Weber described the typical profile of the entrepreneur, which has not changed much over time: "The ideal type of the capitalistic entrepreneur, as it has been represented even in Germany by occasional outstanding examples, has no relation to such more or less refined climbers. He avoids ostentation and unnecessary expenditure, as well as conscious enjoyment of his power, and is embarrassed by the outward signs of the social recognition which he receives. His manner of life is, in other words, often [...] distinguished by a certain ascetic tendency [...]. It is, namely, by no means exceptional, but rather the rule, for him to have a sort of modesty which is essentially more honest than the reserve which Franklin so shrewdly recommends. He gets nothing out of his wealth for himself, except the irrational sense of having done his job well".[12]

Trained Government Official

Max Weber considered that: "The trained official [is] the pillar of both the modern State and of the economic life of the West".[13] Note that the author did not use the term bureaucrat, but trained government official, whom he described thus: "He forms a type of which there have heretofore only been suggestions, which have never remotely approached its present importance for the social order. Of course, the official, even the specialized official, is a very old constituent of the most various societies. But no country and no age has ever experienced, in the same sense as the modern Occident, the absolute and complete dependence of its whole existence, of the political, technical, and economic conditions of its life, on a specially trained organization of officials. The most important functions of the everyday life of society have come to be in the hands of technically, commercially, and above all legally trained government officials".[14]

[11] *The Protestant Ethic and the Spirit of Capitalism.*

[12] Weber, Max (1904–1905), *The Protestant Ethic and the Spirit of Capitalism*, English version translated by Parsons, Talcott (1930), George Allen & Unwin Ltd.

[13] Ibid.

[14] Ibid.

Trade

The economist Friedrich List [1789–1846], though a protectionist, campaigned for the abolition of customs barriers within the German Confederation because they were causing Germany to lose ground to the economies of other nations: "In truth, whereas the other nations cultivate the sciences and the arts from whence trade and industry flourish, the German merchant and manufacturer must today devote a large part of his time to the study of customs-duties and tolls".

What Friedrich List campaigned for in Germany, the European Union secured with the creation of the single market.

In *Zum ewigen Frieden*[15] published in 1795, Immanuel Kant [1724–1804] wrote that: "The spirit of trade cannot coexist with war, and sooner or later this spirit dominates every people".

In *Das Nationale System der politischen Ökonomie*[16] published in 1841, Friedrich List explained that: "International trade, by rousing activity and energy, by the new wants it creates, by the propagation among nations of new ideas and discoveries, and by the diffusion of power, is one of the mightiest instruments of civilization, and one of the most powerful agencies in promoting national prosperity".[17]

Taxation

For Albert Einstein [1879–1955]: "The hardest thing to understand in the world is the income tax".

Inflation

German economist Otto Karl Pöhl [1929–2014], who was the President of the Bundesbank from 1980 to 1991, famously said: "Inflation is like toothpaste. Once it's out, you can hardly get it back in again. So the best thing is not to squeeze too hard on the tube".[18]

---

[15] *Perpetual Peace: A Philosophical Essay.*

[16] *National System of Political Economy.*

[17] List, Friedrich (1841), *National System of Political Economy*, translated from the German by G.A. Matile, Philadelphia: J.B. Lippincott & Co.

[18] Dr. Karl Otto Pöhl, https://www.bundesbank.de/resource/blob/666662/cebdc3a25107a0d45060fdb36270abb4/mL/quotes-by-karl-otto-poehl-data.pdf

Investment

As declared by Helmut Schmidt, who served as Germany's Finance Minister and then, from 1974 to 1982, as its Chancellor: "The profits of today are the investments of tomorrow and the investments of tomorrow make the employment of the day after tomorrow".[19]

Public Spending

In *Grundlegung der politischen Ökonomie,*[20] Adolph Wagner [1835–1917] wrote: "Comparisons in time and space show that in the case of civilised people on the road of progress, there is a steady development in the activity of state and public activities. The more civilised society becomes, the more spendthrift the state becomes".

There follows that: "An ever greater and more important proportion of the collective needs of civilised people in progress are met by the state".

Economic Dynamics

Rudiger Dornbusch [1942–2002] warned: "In economics, things take longer to happen than you think they will, and then they happen faster than you thought they could".

Technique

In a quote widely but not authoritatively attributed to Albert Einstein, the physicist warned: "I fear the day that technology will surpass our human interaction. The world will have a generation of idiots".

[19] Schmidt Helmut, speech delivered on 3 November 1974.

[20] *The Fundamentals of Political Economy.*

Sovereign Debt

In *Das Nationale System der politischen Ökonomie*[21] published in 1841, Friedrich List wrote: "The debts of the State are bills of exchange, which the present draws upon a future generation. They may have been contracted for the particular interest of the present or for that of the future, or for the common benefit of both. In the first case only are they to be condemned".[22]

[21] *National System of Political Economy.*

[22] List, Friedrich (1841), *National System of Political Economy*, translated from the German by G.A. Matile, Philadelphia: J.B. Lippincott & Co.

Romania

Ecology

In *La décroissance. Entropie, écologie, économie*[1] published in 1995, Nicolae Georgescu [1906–1994] concluded: "All is unfolding as if the human species has chosen to lead a short but exciting life, leaving less ambitious species to lead a long but monotonous existence".

The work of Nicolae Georgescu has inspired the degrowth movement.

Corruption

In *Opera politica,*[2] the greatest Romanian romantic poet, Mihai Eminescu [1850–1889] wrote: "What becomes a habit to earn money easily and without work, to set oneself up as a great man without merit - this is the definition of true corruption, the consequences of which are hatred and jealousy of all true merit, resulting in the promotion of these nonentities to those places that should of right be reserved for high intelligence or extraordinary character".[3]

Adding: "There is nothing more dangerous for the conscience of a people than the sight of corruption, of mediocrity rewarded and of demerit elevated".[4]

[1] *Degrowth. Entropy, Ecology, Economy,* translated from the French text, Georgescu-Roegen, N. (2006), *La décroissance. Entropie, écologie, économie*, Paris: Éditions Sang de la terre.

[2] *Political Work.*

[3] Mihai Eminescu, *Opera politica*, II, p.461.

[4] Ibid.

C. Peicuti, *The European Economy in 100 Quotes*, Contributions to Economics,
https://doi.org/10.1007/978-3-031-68819-5_7

And finally: "For the people, poverty leads to corruption more often than wealth".[5]

Wealth

In *Divanul sau Gâlceava înţeleptului cu lumea sau Giudeţul sufletului cu trupul,*[6] Dimitrie Cantemir [1673–1723], one of the greatest linguists of his time, wrote: "The rich man will settle himself in the highest chair." And warned: "When amassing riches, don't let your heart turn to stone".

In the *Cocoşul negru,*[7] the academician Victor Eftimiu [1889–1972] considered that:

> Gold means power, wealth...
> It is the soul of life. The magical key
> That opens the closed door,
> Found everywhere: in the thief's den,
> On the immaculate cloth of the holy altar...
> With gold, you can build a house...a hundred houses...a city
> If you desire, you can defeat a king, buy an enemy. [...]
> For a handful of gold, the honest adviser will
> Sell his emperor and his nation - in the end,
> With a little gold that shines,
> Like stars on the surface of the lake, if you know how,
> You can, through an archangel, even lie to God,
> And his son buy with a handful of silver!
> And the day when Satan, cast out a second time,
> Removed from this earth, will be forced to die -
> He again finds a way to be immortal,
> For gold remains his heir![8]

Enterprise

According to Emil Cioran [1911–1995]: "Not the fear of effort but the fear of success explains more than one failure".

---

[5] Ibid.

[6] *The Divan or the Sage's Dispute with the World.*

[7] *Black Rooster.*

[8] N. Grigorie-Lăcrita, Universul fiscalităţii: [în parodii, pamflete, amuzamente, maxime, cugetări, aforisme, citate, poezii, politică, societate, ştiinţă, Biblie], Bucureşti, Tribuna Economică, 2017, p.188: tab. + 1 CD-ROM Cota: III-322.797, *Cocoşul negru*, Victor Eftimiu, p.119.

Echoing a Latin saying: *Astra inclinant non necessitant* ("Starts incline, they do not compel"), Emil Cioran wrote: "It is not elegant to abuse of misfortune: some individuals, like some peoples, take such delight in it that they dishonour tragedy".

As for Nicolae Titulescu [1882–1941], he wrote: "Destiny is the excuse of the weak and the doing of the strong".

A political and diplomat, he was at various times ambassador, finance minister, and foreign minister between 1927 and 1936. He served two terms as the president of the General Assembly of the League of Nations from 1930 to 1932, for which reason he was one of the characters in Albert Cohen's novel, *La Belle du Seigneur*, in which he was described as the "the beardless guardian of the inner sanctums".[9]

Money

There is a popular Romanian saying, often cited: "Money is the devil's eye".

Prompting this reply from the Romanian philosopher and economist Petre Tutea [1902–1991]: "I don't hate the bourgeoisie. I have come to the conclusion that a man who wants to be rich is not a sinner. An old priest once said: there's a popular saying that money is the devil's eye. I don't see it that way but as a stepladder. If you have money, no matter the amount, and you climb the ladder being a benefactor, it is no longer the devil's eye. And if you step down the ladder, then you take your money with you to hell, succumbing to vices, greed and all the imperfections linked to pride and the desire to be master".

One of the key figures in the 1848 revolution in Iasi, who would go on to serve as Romania's first Foreign Affairs Minister and was one of the founders of the Romanian Academy, the poet Vasile Alecsandri [1821–1890] considered that: "Money is human nature's greatest stumbling block". Adding: "Money, the little wheels that set the world's big wheel in motion".

In *Noapte de Noiembrie,*[10] the poet Alexandru Macedonski [1854–1920] wrote:

> The lure of money!... A saga of so many thousands of years,
> The Divine Comedy with as title: Money!
> A poem of love, pain and pleasure,
> With Paradise rising and Hell falling;
> Gain, which rises on the same pedestal,
> Always moral, eternally immoral.

---

[9]Cohen, Albert (1995), *La belle du seigneur*, translated and with an introduction by David Coward (1995), Penguin Books. First published in France in 1968 by Editions Gallimard.

[10]*November Night.*

Gain, which tramples on virtue and law,
Arrogantly, it advances towards its kingly throne,
And entering triumphantly into the Temple of Wealth,
With the laughter of money under the vaults it sits down
And the yellow of the coin of which it is made
Bears down on the world, keeping it underfoot.[11]

Establishment

Romantic poet, dramatist, and diplomat Vasile Alecsandri wrote: "The bestowing of honours is suffocating for the air is tainted by baseness and flattery".

Work

Romanian Romantic poet, novelist, and journalist Mihai Eminescu considered that: "The reality of work, resulting from the conditions imposed by the political economy, with necessarily an excess of production over consumption, alone resists all crises and all upheavals, and only on the reality of this work can any serious institution be based".[12]

Mihai Eminescu drew attention to the fact that: "No matter how much suet a farmer has, he has no money, and the modern state needs money. Every step a Member of Parliament takes in the House, every stupid thing he says, costs the country money, and money means work. A line written by a subordinate of a subordinate of a village mayor costs money, and money means work. A bad university lecture costs money, and money means work. Well, money is everywhere clearly the embodiment and consequence of work: it is soaked in perspiration, fashioned by physical exertion, and just as the hand of a watch indicates precisely how many hours have passed, the sum in my pocket shows how much human society has toiled for me".[13]

[11] N. Grigorie-Lăcrita, Universul fiscalității: [în parodii, pamflete, amuzamente, maxime, cugetări, aforisme, citate, poezii, politică, societate, ştiinţă, Biblie], Bucureşti, Tribuna Economică, 2017, p. 188: tab. + 1 CD-ROM Cota: III-322.797, *Noapte de Noiembrie*, Alexandru Macedonski, p. 118.

[12] *Timpul, Le journal Le temps*, 30 April 1880.

[13] *Opera politica*, I, 331.

Savings

Mihai Eminescu defined savings as follows: "Savings, that is the proper measurement of the benefits brought by a certain expenditure and the sacrifices made to this end; this applies both to the general government economy and individual economy".[14]

In 1921, Nicolae Titulescu explained: "Savings: the result of a reduction in expenditures. Sobriety: the result of a reduction in consumption".[15]

Poverty

Mihai Eminescu explained that poverty is a scourge not just for the individual but also for the economy as a whole: "Poverty is a source of physical and moral ills, but it is also true that moral maladies are in turn the cause of economic decadence".[16]

In the speech, *Progress in the Idea of Peace*, given in Cambridge on 19 November 1930, Nicolae Titulescu asked: "What can economic misery produce if not war or disorder?"

Deficit

According to Nicolae Titulescu: "There is no monetary stability as long as there is a fiscal deficit", and "Balancing expenditures and receipts is the key to financial recovery".[17]

Confidence

Nicolae Titulescu considered that: "Confidence is not established by speeches, especially in financial matters, but by the existence of appropriate institutions".[18]

---

[14] Mihai Eminescu, *Opera politica*, I, 61.

[15] *Discursul Dlui N. Titulescu în discutia generala a Legii contributiilor directe*, 10 iunie 1921, Bucuresti.

[16] Mihai Eminescu, *Opera politica*, II, 347.

[17] Nicolae Titulescu, *Documents diplomatiques*, 21 June 1932, Lausanne.

[18] Ibid.

Gifts

Dimitrie Cantemir invites the reader to: “Apply gifts you have received in the service of good, not bad deeds”.

Hungary

Game Theory

János Harsanyi [1920–2000] shared the 1994 Sveriges Riksbank Prize in Economic Sciences in Memory of Alfred Nobel with John Nash [1928–2015] and Reinhard Selten [1930–2016] "for their pioneering analysis of equilibria in the theory of non-cooperative games". The Nobel Committee declared on this occasion that the game theory had profoundly renewed the analysis of markets, the behaviour and strategies of players, the different forms of competition, and market typologies.

About how János Harsanyi came to economics: in 1944, he had to join a forced labour unit because of his Jewish origins, but managed to escape, narrowly avoiding deportation to a concentration camp. In 1947, he defended his philosophy thesis and went on to study sociology, before fleeing Communist Hungary and emigrating to Australia. As his qualifications were not recognised, he studied economics and published scientific articles whilst working in a factory. Thanks to a scholarship, he emigrated to the United States.

Game theory is to predict the behaviour of economic agents on the basis of the hypothesis that every agent always makes rational choices aimed at maximising his expected gains and minimising his expected losses.

John Nash focused his research on games in which the players know each others' preferences. In 1967, János Harsanyi expanded the work of John Nash to "games of incomplete information". From 1966 to 1968, he was part of a team of game theorists tasked with advising the United States Arms Control and Disarmament Agency during the Soviet Union–US disarmament talks. His participation in these games of incomplete information as a consultant required that he devise a solution.

C. Peicuti, *The European Economy in 100 Quotes*, Contributions to Economics,
https://doi.org/10.1007/978-3-031-68819-5_8

For Harsanyi: "In principle, every social situation involves strategic interaction among the participants. Thus, one might argue that proper understanding of any social situation would require game-theoretic analysis".[1]

According to him: "It is our common experience as human beings that the results of social forces seem to admit only of probabilistic predictions".[2]

In the context of cooperative games, the economist proposed a solution, which has gone on to be known as the Harsanyi value. Harsanyi managed to find solutions to the various "games" he faced that would have defeated more than one, enabling him not only to survive but also to win the Nobel Prize. A virtuoso. A case of: "To be, or not to be, that is the question".

Regarding his approach to games, he had this to say: "I haven't played a chess match for several decades. At one point I lost most of my chess games. Then I realized many of my competitors were memorizing the best moves and I was unwilling to do this".

Would-be grandmasters be warned!

Innovation

Dennis Gabor [1900–1979], who was awarded the 1971 Nobel Prize in Physics "for his invention and development of the holographic method", considered that: "All that can be accomplished technically will be accomplished".

Credit

Endre Ady [1877–1919] contended that: "People are two kinds. Either they are loan sharks or they want to be loan sharks. Money and commodity usury are just two types of widespread usury. [...] The greatest usurer is life, which takes a terrible interest for the little pleasure it gives...".[3]

---

[1] Harsanyi, János (1994), *Games with Incomplete Information*, Nobel Lecture, https://www.nobelprize.org/uploads/2018/06/harsanyi-lecture.pdf

[2] Ibid.

[3] Ady, Endre (1901), *A hétről (About the Week)*, in Nagyváradi Napló (Journal of Oradea).

A few words of advice from Ferenc Móra [1879–1934]: "If you want to borrow money, make people believe that you have money".[4]

Poverty

Kelemen Mikes [1690–1761] observed: "Usually the poor catch the bird and the rich eat it".[5]

As for Sándor Márai [1900–1989], he had this to say: "Poverty is usually best dealt with from a distance from a high philosophical point of view, all the more so because if one deals with poverty in a more practical tone and perspective, it is internationally agreed that in most civilised states you will sooner or later be closed down".[6]

According to György Bálint [1906–1943]: "The essence of poverty is therefore exploitation and, as a consequence, total vulnerability. Poor people are always dependent on other people, and their lives are a daily struggle to survive".[7]

According to the journalist and literary critic: "Today I am no longer afraid of beggars. When I see them, I feel a different feeling: shame. I feel ashamed when I throw alms into outstretched palms, and ashamed when I give nothing. I am ashamed as soon as I see them - I am simply ashamed that they are in the world, a world in which I have a place, and which I have had little success in changing".[8]

According to Albert Szent-Györgyi [1893–1986]: "The rich are those who have more money than they desire and the poor are those who have more desire than money. The unskilled worker of today has more money than the princes of a few centuries ago. What makes us poor is the desire for more. The secret to happiness is not to get more, but to be happy with what we have and to fill the empty spaces in our lives rather than expanding them".[9]

---

[4]Móra, Ferenc (1969), *Bolondságok, enyimek is, máséi is (Follies, both mine and others')*, Budapest.

[5]Mikes, Kelemen (2011), *Lettres de Turquie (Letters from Turkey)*, Paris, Honoré Champion, 2011.

[6]Márai, Sándor (1933), *Un szegények iskolája (School for the Poor)*, Budapest.

[7]Bálint, György (1969), *Gondos Ernő*, Budapest.

[8]Ibid.

[9]Szent-Györgyi, Albert (1988), *Kis katekizmus (Small catechism)*, in Válogatott tanulmányok (Chosen Studies), p. 310.

Ferenc Móra believed that poverty could be eradicated: "If people spent a quarter as much on doing good to others as they do on doing harm to themselves, there would be no trace of poverty".[10]

Money

The great poet Sándor Petőfi [1823–1849] wrote: "The sea is the money in which it sinks. Many ships: principle, character, honour".[11]

József Eötvös [1813–1871] provided a damming assessment: "Nowadays, people sacrifice even their prejudices for money. This is the measure of its immense power".[12]

József Attila [1905–1937] considered that: "In a constitutional state, money is the weapon".[13]

Mór Jókai [1825–1904] analysed man's relationship with money through linguistics: "The Hungarian 'earns' money, the German 'deserves' money (geld verdienen), the French 'wins' money (gagner de l'argent), and the American 'makes' money. Perfectly typical terms. The poor Hungarian, one sees, as it were, how he looks for money, in which bush he may find it; the pious German, how he sweats, works hand and foot, till he earns that piece of money; the light-blooded Frenchman, how he risks and wins, if he finds another who loses; while the heavy-blooded Yankee sits still, and, clipping his nails, makes money".[14]

Mór Jókai wrote: "Many great men have a 'lot' of money: but only the poor man usually has 'enough' money".[15]

Frigyes Karinthy [1887–1938] stated: "Rockefeller and I have one thing in common - he has money, I don't".[16]

---

[10] Móra, Ferenc (1969), *Bolondságok, enyimek is, máséi is (Follies, both mine and others')*, p. 83.

[11] Petőfi, Sándor (2008), *Verstár: ötven költő összes verse (Verstár: all poems by fifty poets)*, Budapest.

[12] Eötvös, József (1977), *Vallomások és gondolatok (Testimonies and reflections)*, Miklós Bényei, Budapest, p. 752.

[13] Attila, József (2006), *Gyönyörűt láttam (I saw beauty)*, in József Attila összes versei (All poems by Attila József), Budapest, p. 506.

[14] Jókai, Mór (1924), *Jókai breviárium (Jókai's Breviary)*, Budapest, p. 197.

[15] Ibid, p. 204.

[16] Karinthy, Frigyes (1964), *Naplóm, életem (My Diary, my Life)*, Budapest, p. 278.

György Moldova [1934–2022] said: "I do not believe that the interests of the poor can be represented by billionaires".[17]

Tibor Déry [1894–1977] wrote that: "The rich can always toy with the poor, because they have the money, that is, the power".[18]

Ferenc Deák [1803–1876] contended that: "Power is only a means; the end is the happiness of the people".[19]

According to Sándor Márai: "If we look hard enough, we see that money can indeed buy everything in the world, from sheep's milk to unreserved lust to the stock surplus of the underground railway, and we readily admit that the possibilities of possession and satisfaction through money are not small. But money cannot buy, for example, the ability of a stupid man to think, even with money - and let us admit that thinking is more amusing than champagne with women in some fashionable Marseilles public house - money cannot neutralise the fear of death, nor can money buy such simple abilities as the ability to sing or a sense of humour".[20]

Inflation

For Albert Szent-Györgyi: "Most of the time, inflation is nothing more than a form of massive robbery by the government; the government spends what the citizen has saved".[21]

Nicholas Kaldor [1908–1986] drew attention to the fact that: "the problem of keeping inflation at bay will increasingly be at the centre of preoccupations of all industrialized countries, with untoward consequences in terms of waste of resources and unemployment".[22]

---

[17] Györgyi, Orbán (2014), *Nincs magyar baloldal, a baloldal én vagyok (There is no Hungarian left, the Left is Me)*, Origo, 2014, available at: https://www.origo.hu/kultura/20141212-interju-moldova-gyorggyel.html

[18] Déry, Tibor (1977), *A félfülű (The one-eared man)*, in A gyilkos és én. Kisregények (The killer and Me. Short Stories), Budapest, p. 193.

[19] Deák Ferenc, *Deák Ferenc 1861-iki első felirati beszéde (Ferenc Deák's first speech in 1861)*, Budapest, 1898, p. 6.

[20] Márai, Sándor, (1933), *Un szegények iskolája (School for the Poor)*, Budapest.

[21] Szent-Györgyi, Albert (1988), *Kis katekizmus (Small catechism)*, in Válogatott tanulmányok (Chosen Studies), p. 308.

[22] Kaldor, Nicholas (1976), *Inflation and Recession in the World Economy*, The Economic Journal Vol. 86, No. 344 (December 1976), Oxford University Press.

Paper Money

Zsigmond Móricz [1879–1942] considered that: "This horrible invention, paper money, has destroyed the value of wealth, its honour; it revolves fast, a great mass, it is quickly exchanged, it comes, it goes, it is a breeze: it makes all life so transitory...".[23]

Capitalism

According to Arthur Koestler [1905–1983]: "Capitalism is the exploitation of man by man. Socialism is the exact opposite".

Power

For Lajos Kossuth [1802–1894]: "Knowing that others are even more cowardly than us is the great secret of power".[24]

[23] Móricz, Zsigmond (2003), *Giotto és Rafael (Giotto and Rafael)*, in Móricz Zsigmond novellák III (Móricz Zsigmond novellák III), Budapest, Osiris Classics, p. 21.

[24] Kossuth, Lajos (1966), *Kossuth összes munkái 6. Ifjúkori iratok (All the works of Kossuth 6)*, in Törvényhatósági tudósítások (Reports from the Law Courts), p. 184.

Czech Republic

Budget

According to Joseph A. Schumpeter [1883–1950]: "It is Goldscheid's enduring merit to have been the first to have laid proper stress on this way of looking at fiscal history: to have broadcast the truth that 'the budget is the skeleton of the state stripped of all misleading ideologies'—a collection of hard, naked facts which yet remain to be drawn into the realm of sociology".[1]

Innovation

In *The Theory of Economic Development* published in 1941, Joseph A. Schumpeter, who was a lifelong defender of competition, warned that: "The introduction of new methods of production and new commodities is hardly conceivable with perfect - and perfectly prompt - competition from the start".[2]

The *Manufacture royale de glaces de miroirs* (later Saint-Gobain) was started up to stem imports from Venice and it produced all 357 mirrors in the Hall of Mirrors of the Palace of Versailles. Airbus was created to rival Boeing. All these ventures needed a helping hand from the State, the case also for the Internet.

---

[1] Schumpeter, Joseph A. (1918), *The crisis of the Tax State*, enlarged version of a lecture Schumpeter gave before the Wiener Soziologische Gesellschaft, published in 1918 under the title *Die Krise der Steuerstaates* as issue number 4 of Zeiqragen azu dem Gebiet der Soziologie, an English translation, by Wolfgang F. Stolper and Richard A. Musgrave, appeared (1954) in International Economic Papers (n.4).

[2] Schumpeter, Joseph A. (1941), *The Theory of Economic Development*, new edition published 1980, Routledge.

C. Peicuti, *The European Economy in 100 Quotes*, Contributions to Economics,
https://doi.org/10.1007/978-3-031-68819-5_9

For Joseph A. Schumpeter innovation referred to: "The process of industrial mutation - if I may use that biological term - that incessantly revolutionizes the economic structure from within, incessantly destroying the old one, incessantly creating a new one. This process of Creative Destruction is the essential fact about capitalism".[3]

Cycles

Joseph A. Schumpeter explained that cycles were inherent to the market economy: "Cycles are not, like tonsils, separable things that might be treated by themselves, but are, like the beat of the heart, of the essence of the organism that displays them".[4]

Capitalism

In *Capitalism, Socialism and Democracy*, Joseph A. Schumpeter wrote: "Historically, the modern democracy rose along with capitalism, and in causal connection with it".[5] He added: "Modern pacifism and modern international morality are nonetheless products of capitalism".[6]

Entrepreneur

In *Capitalism, Socialism and Democracy*, Joseph A. Schumpeter defined the entrepreneur as follows: "The function of entrepreneurs is to reform or revolutionize the pattern of production by exploiting an invention or, more generally, an untried technological possibility for producing a new commodity or producing an old one in a new way, by opening up a new source of supply of materials or a new outlet for products, by reorganizing an industry and so on".[7]

---

[3]Schumpeter, Joseph A. (1942), *Capitalism, Socialism and Democracy*, Harper and Brother New York.

[4]Schumpeter, Joseph A. (1923), *Business Cycles.* McGraw-Hill Book Company New York.

[5]Schumpeter, Joseph A. (1942), *Capitalism, Socialism and Democracy*, Harper and Brother New York.

[6]Ibid.

[7]Ibid.

Inflation

In *Capitalism, Socialism and Democracy*, Joseph A. Schumpeter assimilated inflation to monetary expropriation: "Inflation expropriates the holder of claims in terms of money in a delightfully simple way".[8]

Debt

As underlined by Joseph A. Schumpeter: "[The entrepreneur] can only become an entrepreneur by previously becoming a debtor".[9]

Progress

Franz Kafka [1883–1924] observed that: "Believing in progress does not mean believing that any progress has yet been made".

Wealth

Franz Kafka asked: "What is wealth? For one, an old shirt is already wealth. Another is poor with ten million. Wealth is something completely relative and unsatisfactory".

There is a popular Czech saying that: "Wealth gives rise to envy, poverty to hatred".

Poverty

There is a Czech saying that: "When poverty comes in at the door, love flies out at the window".

[8] Ibid.

[9] Schumpeter, Joseph A. (1949), *The Theory Of Economic Development*, Harvard University Press.

Brand Image

The famous writer Milan Kundera [1929–2023], whose novels explored the "unbearable lightness of being" and the meaning of life, stated: "Having long been the brain of Europe, Paris is still today the capital of something more than France".[10]

Utility

Milan Kundera said ironically: "What does it really mean to be useful? Today's world, just as it is, contains the sum of the utility of all people of all times. Which implies: the highest morality consists in being useless".[11]

Market Economy

About communism, Milan Kundera wrote: "Private and public are two essentially different worlds and that respect for that difference is the indispensable condition, the sine qua non, for a man to live free".[12]

In other words, neither the market economy nor the command economy can guarantee man's freedom.

Money

The Czech artist Vladimír Rencin [1941–2017] wrote: "Money won't make you happy, but everybody wants to find out for themselves".

Philosopher Johann Amos Comenius [1592–1670] warned: "Money leaves you more easily than it came".

There's a saying that: "If you want to lose a friend, lend them money".

Another is that: "In modern times, even a king is safer with dollars in his pockets than a crown on his head".

---

[10] Interview given to Antoine de Gaudemar, February 1984.

[11] Kundera, Milan (1999), *Immortality*, Harper Perennial

[12] Kundera, Milan (1996), *Testaments Betrayed*, Faber and Faber.

Mathematician Stanislav Komenda [1936–2009] observed that: “Patience runs out more quickly if money runs out too”.

According to Olympic athlete Vladimír Syrovatka [1908–1973]: “It is easier to drown with the pockets full of money”.

On the same subject, still according to Vladimír Syrovatka:

Unlike good deeds, bad ones can be expressed with money.

Money makes a good means but a bad goal.

And

In America, time is not money; in America, everything is money.

There’s a popular saying that: “What’s easily won is easily lost”.

Interest Rates

Eugen von Böhm-Bawerk [1851–1914] in *Positive Theorie des Kapitals*[13] published in 1889, had this to say about interest: “I do not see that there is anything objectionable in this. For natural reasons, present goods are certainly more valuable commodities than future goods”.[14]

Value

According to Vladimír Syrovatka: “Everything of value is a result of effort”.

The same Vladimír Syrovatka considered that: “Poverty is a good place to discover true values”.

Ecology

Vladimír Syrovatka estimated that: “Where the economy blooms, flowers wilt”.

[13] *The Positive Theory of Capital.*

[14] Böhm-Bawerk, Eugen von (1930), *The Positive Theory of Capital*, translated with a preface and analysis by William Smart, G. E. Stechert & Co., New York, https://mises.org/library/positive-theory-capital

According to Vladimír Syrovatka: "That it is possible to have unlimited economic growth on a limited planet is an idea only an economist, politician or a madman could come up with".

Concerning our attitude to climate change, Vladimír Syrovatka wrote: "Our consumerist paradise can be compared to the Titanic; there is still dancing on the upper decks".

Industrialisation

Vladimír Syrovatka wrote that: "The world industrialisation should have brought everlasting peace; but industry requires resources that need to be fought for".

Globalisation

Still according to Vladimír Syrovatka: "All attempts at globalisation, including the modern one, are built on the same premise: stealing from our neighbours".

Corruption

Vladimír Syrovatka observed that: "Connecting politics with business is a trick where the state gets poorer and the politicians get richer".

As to what constitutes a profitable investment, Czech accordionist, singer, humourist, and cartoonist Miroslav Kemel [1963–] concluded that: "According to all indexes, the safest option is still to invest into corruption".

Economics

Czech economist Tomáš Sedláček [1977–] explains that: "Economics is a belief like all others. To me, one of the biggest acts of heresy in modern times is the conviction that something does not come from a belief. That something is absolutely real and true".

Time

Actor, playwright, and writer Jan Werich [1905–1980] wrote that: “People created time to know from what time till when and what they get for it”.

Trade

Tomáš Baťa [1876–1932], the Czech entrepreneur and founder of the Bata shoe company, considered that: “A good trade is one where everyone involved is happy”.

He also said: “If you want to build a big business, first build yourself”; and that “Each human activity will somehow project into the numbers”.

Estonia

Money

The quotation below is taken from the second volume of the pentalogy of short stories *Truth and Justice*, a major work by Estonian writer, playwright, and essayist Anton Hansen Tammsaare [1878–1940]:

He [Mr. Maurus, school director] says: "Don't ever put money in a box, not here, nor in a hotel, but bring it to Mr. Maurus. Those who don't know how to handle their own money should bring it to me. Come even in the middle of the night, come and knock at my door, you see, like this: knock, knock, knock!—but not with your fist, so that the whole house wakes up—understand? For Mr. Maurus is never asleep when someone's bringing him money. He puts the money in the book—then it's safe. A person will die, a book will not...".[1]

Homeless People

Juhan Liiv [1864–1913] is one of Estonia's best-known and best-loved poets. In 1905, he wrote the poem Homeless Man:

I came from town. Snowfall.
Not a job to be found.
Snowfall. My feet are tired.
I was hungry, hungry.[2]

[1] Tammsaare, Anton Hansen (1929), Indrek: Vol. II, *Truth and Justice - A Pentalogy*, translated by Chris Moseley and Matthew Hyde.

[2] Liiv, Juhan (1905), *Homeless Man*, translated by Jüri Talvet and H. L. Hix.

C. Peicuti, *The European Economy in 100 Quotes*, Contributions to Economics,
https://doi.org/10.1007/978-3-031-68819-5_10

Inequalities

Writer, film director, and statesman Lennart Meri [1929–2006], who was President of Estonia from 1992 to 2001, has this to say in 2001: "The most effective way to reduce social inequality is to invest in education".

In 2008, historian Jaak Valge [1955–] stated: "For example, Estonia between the two world wars was a socially and economically very homogenous country, the gap between the richest and the poorest tenth of the population was much smaller than it is today. Stratification has increased worldwide in the last few decades".

Provident State

Lennart Meri said: "The Estonian state is expensive and the Estonian state is dear. It is expensive on the citizen's wallet and it is dear to the citizen's heart".

Economic Reform

In 1998, Lennart Meri stated: "Economic reform is, in simple language, a redistribution of assets. It has always been a dirty time everywhere".

Crisis

In 1997, Lennart Meri explained that: "The situation is shit, but it is the fertilizer for our future".

In 1932, Joakim Puhk [1888–1942], the founder of the Estonian Chamber of Commerce and Industry, stated: "Our economic situation is difficult, but we can overcome it if we stick to the set targets and the fundamentals of economic life. Jumping from one extreme to another is dangerous, especially in times of economic crisis, which are similar in nature to economic war".

In 2020, Rainer Kattel [1974–], a Professor of Innovation and Public Governance at University College London, declared: "The global crisis shows that innovation is political: who, how and with what means creates new opportunities is not a law of nature, but a joint decision of all of us. For more than 10 years, the Estonian government has been trying to direct research and development funds to alleviate societal challenges. To no avail so far, because we see our problems too narrowly.

We need to be able to be in dialogue with the world's changing innovation debate, which in the post-corona era is likely to be less and less the face of the wealthy white man".

International Value Creation Chains

Erik Terk [1952–], Director at the Estonian Institute for Futures Studies, Tallinn University, explained in 2019: "The problem of the Estonian economy is not so much a lack of innovation, but rather a poor position in international value creation chains".

Work

In 2016, Andrus Kivirähk [1970–], one of Estonia's most famous writers, many of whose works have been adapted to the screen, wrote: "It is not possible to work only when the mood strikes. The mood doesn't come by itself, the mood has to be created, and the only way to do that is to sit down at the computer and start working".

Digitalisation

Estonia has been a forerunner in Europe when it comes to digital transformation.

In 2021, Meelis Kitsing [1973–], a Professor of Political Economy and Rector of the Estonian Business School, stated: "Different from several EU countries, digital interactions have become embedded in Estonia, for example. Some of these services are easily understandable, such as Internet banking which Estonians have enjoyed since 1996. Others are unique to the outside world, such as internet voting, which has been available since 2005 and is used by almost half of voters. Some are invisible but fundamental for the ecosystem—such as the X-Road—which, as the backbone of digital infrastructure, facilitates data sharing among public and private organizations. Digitalization in Estonia has been an evolutionary process where key decisions about the delivery of services and digital identity were already made 20 years ago. However, this process is also characterized by a high degree of heterogeneity".

In 2018, Raul Eamets [1964–], an economist and the Dean of the Faculty of Social Science at Tartu University, predicted that: "Convergence of technologies [...] (biotechnology, IT applications, nanotechnology, etc.) will increase in value. Digitisation of production, automation and 3D printing are also becoming an inevitable part of the traditional economy. Big data and the possibilities arising from its processing are a separate field".

Doing Business

Eduard Vilde [1865–1933] is one of the most revered figures in Estonian literature and the author of many classics, including Pisuhänd, a comedy about social ascension in the country's intellectual and financial circles. One of the characters in this comedy, Piibeleht, explains that: "Business is not to be ashamed".

Continuous Learning

In 2023, the economist Urmas Varblane [1961–] delivered the following analysis: "Continuous learning is the basis of all changes and the success of the Estonian economy".

State Strategy

Urmas Varblane had this to say: "A successful country has a whole range of abilities, which Estonia could also strive to possess. The most important thing is to be strategic and adaptable. As a small country, Estonia cannot afford short-term decisions. The ability to respond quickly and appropriately to changes in the environment around us requires strategic thinking at the level of the state, companies and every citizen. We should observe global strategic developments much more, pay attention to where the centre of gravity of the world economy is moving and shape our strategies accordingly. We would need more statesmanship, and the ability to foresee the consequences of our decisions. But it also means being able to see the consequences of your omissions".

PhD Holders

In 2014, Kadri Ukrainski [1974], Professor of Research and Innovation Policy at the University of Tartu, stated: "If we want to play in the top league, our companies and state institutions should also have top league capability, which, among other things, keeps people with doctorate degrees in the team. In Estonian society, it is necessary to make wise decisions, before which decisions must also discussed with scientists and their analytical ability used".

In contrast the United States, and with the exception of Germany, PhD holders are not given their rightful place in the European Union, seriously damaging its competitiveness.

Liberalism

The economist, human geographer, and politician Kalev Kukk [1951–] explained that when Estonia gained independence in 1991: "The common belief of most political forces was formed that Estonia's economic success can only be based on openness, i.e. to the establishment of a maximally liberal trade regime".

Slovenia

Until indicated otherwise, the quotes below are from the book *Aforizmi*,[1] a collection of aphorisms published by the prolific writer and scriptwriter Žarko Petan [1929–2014].

Small Country

It is a misfortune when a small State has so many great men.

Economist

Even as we drown, gargling is the cure proposed by economists.

Corruption

Good and honest men can also be bought, but you have to pay them a good and honest price.

Inflation

It's not meat that's become dearer, but money that's become less dear.

Die today... tomorrow your funerals will cost even more.

[1] https://plus.cobiss.net/cobiss/si/en/bib/nuk/75573504

C. Peicuti, *The European Economy in 100 Quotes*, Contributions to Economics,
https://doi.org/10.1007/978-3-031-68819-5_11

Brain Drain

Exporting intelligence is not very intelligent.

Socialism

In socialist countries, even crises have been nationalised.

Socialism is a paradise for capitalist tourists.

To demolish things in the name of progress is as senseless as building them in the name of regression.

I'd like to see the building of socialism on this earth finished, but could I please see the blueprints first?

I'm all in favour of a cultural revolution, provided that the revolutionaries are cultured.

State

They strip you of your trousers, and then tell you to tighten your belt.

Is stupidity a monopoly of the State?

Currency

It's ironic that healthy currency seems to come only from sick countries.

Money

Josip Stritar [1836–1923] pointed out that: "Money has a strange power, it attracts everything, it piles up; there will come a time when only a handful of rich people will be left in the world, all the others will be beggars! Money is ruthless!"

The writer warned: "He who has money is master, power and right are his, everything is his; money gives everything, everything his heart desires, and woe to him who falls under his yoke!"

The poet, writer, and playwright Ivan Cankar [1876–1918] made the point that: "With money a man is a master, without money he is a slave".

Poverty

For the philosopher Slavoj Žižek [1949–]: "Poverty is not a lack of money, but a lack of opportunity. Today, you're rich if you own your time".

The writer Franci Zagoričnik [1933–1997] considered that: "Poverty is a silent carpet covering the thorns of wealth".

State

Janez Drnovšek [1950–2008], who served as Slovenia's Prime Minister and then as its President, stated: "Economic progress must be at the service of a better life for all, and not just a handful".

According to Slovene writer, playwright and politician Tone Partljič [1940–]: "The State is not just the holder of power, but also the guardian of the common interest".

Slovenian politician Spomenka Hribar [1941–] said: "The measure of a society is how it looks after its most vulnerable members". He drew attention to the fact that: "There is the possibility that one day this country will start to work for its people".

Maša Stošič asked: "What's the point of our beautiful façades if there is nothing behind them?"

Taxation

For Tone Partljič: "Taxes are a fundamental support for the development of society and for equal opportunities".

Wealth

Slovenian writer Janez Mencinger [1838–1912] observed that: "Wealth in itself does not bring pleasure, but subjects the human spirit to the fleeting power of things".

Tone Partljič considered that: "Wealth without morality is just a bunch of empty numbers".

Positioning

For Andrej Velkavrh [1959–], evolution depends on setting ambitious objectives: "There was a time when we hoped, at least tacitly, to become another Switzerland. If that has not happened, it is because we're aiming far too low".

Risks

Matjaž Gruden urges us to be careful in any undertaking and not take risks without thinking about the consequences: "At a certain point, playing with fire takes on a momentum of its own that can no longer be stopped, not even by the first person to light the torch".

The diplomat echoes the ancient Greeks' view that the beginning does not foreshadow the end. In Herodotus' *Histories*, Artabanus cautioned Xerxes: "A well-laid plan is ever to my mind most profitable; for even though it be thwarted later, yet none the less has the plan been good, and it is but chance that has baffled the design".[2]

Economic Patriotism

The poet Simon Gregorčič [1844–1906] wrote: "What you do for yourself disappears with you. What you do for the nation lives on forever".

[2] Herodotus, *Histories*, Book VII, Loeb Classical Library edition (1922), https://penelope.uchicago.edu/Thayer/E/Roman/Texts/Herodotus/7a*.html

Lithuania

Monetary History

Lithuanian priest, economist, and professor Vladas Jurgutis [1885–1966], who served as the first Chairman of the Bank of Lithuania, and is considered to be the father of the Lithuanian litas, wrote: "Money, that *nervi rerum*, is not only the basis of every private economy, but also of public and national economies, because not only the proper work of the private economy depends on the monetary system, but also the economic, cultural and political well-being of the entire nation [. . .]. In the history of money, as if in a kaleidoscope, not only the history of the state itself but also the history of the entire nation passes by".[1]

Work

Jonas Jablonskis [1860–1930], an eminent linguist, wrote: "Work has no legs, it does not come to us by itself. You have to look for it by yourself everywhere and always".[2]

---

[1] Jurgutis, Vladas (1938), *Pinigai(The Money)*, from *Reikalingi žodžiai: aforizmai, rinktinės mintys (Necessary Words: Aphorisms, Collected Thoughts)*, compiled by Raisa Melnikova, Vilnius: Tyto alba, 2010.

[2] Jablonskis, Jonas (2000), from *Rinktinės mintys: citatos, aforizmai, priežodžiai ir patarlės (Selected Thoughts: Quotes, Aphorisms, Proverbs And Sayings)*, compiled by Juozas Prunskis, second corrected edition, Kaunas: Naujasis amžius.

C. Peicuti, *The European Economy in 100 Quotes*, Contributions to Economics,
https://doi.org/10.1007/978-3-031-68819-5_12

Ownership

The philosopher and educator Stasys Šalkauskis [1886–2004], who was the Rector of Vytautas-Magnus University, made the case that: "Not individual property, as preached by individualism, and not public property, as preached by socialism, but joint property of the individual and society, is most suitable for human life".[3]

The writer and politician Kazimieras Saja [1932–], one of the signatories of the Act of the Re-Establishment of the State of Lithuania in 1990, stated: "The most valuable possession is the one that weighs nothing".[4]

Career

The philosopher and historian of ideas Leonidas Donskis [1962–2016], who was a member of the European Parliament from 2009 to 2014, asked: "What is an immersive career? A dizzyingly fast transition from feeling every moment of your life to planning your life in months and years. In happy families, children are not forced to become adults too quickly and immerse themselves in the prose of life. Thus, in societies where there is no lack of respect for human freedom and spontaneity, young people are not brutally forced into a predictable adult life and forcibly accelerated socialization, a professional career and the creation of success".[5]

Bureaucracy

Leonidas Donskis had questions aplenty: "What is behind the incessant growth of bureaucracy and the ever-increasing belief in that necessity? Nothing more than a fundamental, almost medieval mistrust of the individual, blindly relying on institutional control".[6]

---

[3]Šalkauskis, Stasys (2000), from *Rinktinės mintys: citatos, aforizmai, priežodžiai ir patarlės (Selected Thoughts: Quotes, Aphorisms, Proverbs And Sayings)*, compiled by Juozas Prunskis, second corrected edition, Kaunas: Naujasis amžius.

[4]Saja, Kazimieras, from *Reikalingi žodžiai: aforizmai, rinktinės mintys (Necessary Words: Aphorisms, Collected Thoughts)*, compiled by Raisa Melnikova, Vilnius: Tyto alba, 2010.

[5]Donskis, Leonidas (2010), *Mažasis patirties žemėlapis: mintys ir aforizmai* (A Little Map of Experience: Thoughts and Aphorisms), Vilnius: Versus aureus.

[6]Ibid.

Wellbeing

The journalist and writer Algimantas Čekuolis [1931–] explained: "Now we all know that the well-being of a nation does not depend on the area of the country (example - Russia, Kazakhstan, Argentina, African countries), but on the level of civilization of its inhabitants and the democratic system (Holland, Belgium, Luxembourg, England, current Germany, Scandinavian countries)".[7]

[7]Čekuolis, Algimantas, from *Reikalingi žodžiai: aforizmai, rinktinės mintys (Necessary Words: Aphorisms, Collected Thoughts)*, compiled by Raisa Melnikova, Vilnius: Tyto alba, 2010.

Denmark

Gifts

In *The Two Baronesses,* first published in 1849, the writer of plays, travelogues, novels, and poems Hans Christian Andersen [1805–1875], best remembered for his literary fairy tales, wrote: "Small contributions are received with gratitude, large ones with greed".[1]

National Specificity

Poul Schlüter [1929–2021], Denmark's Prime Minister from 1982 to 1993, stated in 1982: "Denmark is the country where you eat green, vote red and work black".

Masters

A Danish proverb collected in 1682 by the folklorist Peder Syv [1631–1702] says: "All will be masters; no one will carry the sack".

Pay Equality

In 1939, the rector and historian Aagot Lading [1909–1963] demanded: "Equal pay for equal work".

[1] Andersen, H.C (1876): The Two Baronesses, New York, Hurd and Houghton.

C. Peicuti, *The European Economy in 100 Quotes*, Contributions to Economics,
https://doi.org/10.1007/978-3-031-68819-5_13

Taxation

Writer, poet, and philosopher Poul Martin Møller [1794–1838] considered that: "The money is best in the citizens' pockets".

Luxembourg

Wealth

In *Luxembourgeois, qui êtes-vous?* Jul Christophory [1939–] explained that Luxembourg's prosperity stemmed from a mindset: "A small country that was still insanely rich before the Second World War, where the smallest baker, the smallest butcher in the smallest hamlet could afford sumptuous American cars. But it was not capitalism that made the country rich. I think it was a Rabelaisian conception of existence, a simplification of human relationships, perhaps a particular interpretation of the spirit of the law and, above all, a work ethic to behold, for everyone worked themselves to the bone. There was only one beggar in Luxembourg, and he was French...".[1]

In his book *Comment rester ce que nous sommes!* Georges Erasme Muller [1925–2010] poked fun at the rich: "Another tragedy goes unnoticed: that of the rich. No matter how hard they try to waste money, they just can't seem to get any poorer. In vain they buy second, third, and fourth homes in the most exotic locations, visit their American cousins every weekend and give Porsches and Jaguars to their children before they know how to drive. Try as they might, their bank accounts just keep getting fatter and fatter".[2]

Jul Christophory ironises about the greater tolerance afforded to the rich than to the poor:

> The world is a bag full of crayfish
> Clawing at each other

[1] Christophory, Jul (1984), *Luxembourgeois, qui êtes-vous?: échos et chuchotements*, Chap. 8: *Prospérité, Démographie et Piston*, second edition, Luxembourg, G. Binsfeld, p.132.

[2] George Erasmus, Alison Koch-Kent (2002), *Comment rester ce que nous sommes!*, first French translation by Esch/Alzette, Le Phare, p.179.

C. Peicuti, *The European Economy in 100 Quotes*, Contributions to Economics,
https://doi.org/10.1007/978-3-031-68819-5_14

Those above are flushed
Those below are crushed.
Stupid as the rich man may be
His fortune will be
But for the poor devil in his hovel
His foolishness is truly unforgivable[3]

European Union

In his speech *Les institutions européennes* of 15 January 2002, Jean-Claude Juncker [1954–] explained: "If now some people, not versed in history, are quick to circulate the slogan 'In Europe, it is above all the economy that counts', I reply that in Europe the economy is certainly important, but it is not only the economy that counts. The economy is a means to an end, not an end in itself. That's why the economy must be complemented by the social dimension. Europe cannot be built against the will of the workers".[4]

Jean-Claude Juncker added: "I do not want the debate about Europe's future to be reduced to a debate about the reform of the EU institutions".

And went on: "East to West: Europe must breathe with both lungs. Otherwise our continent will struggle for air".[5]

Concerning Brexit, Jean-Claude Juncker considered that: "On 29 March 2019, the United Kingdom will leave the European Union. This will be both a sad and tragic moment. We will always regret it. But we have to respect the will of the British people. We will advance, we must advance because Brexit is not everything. Because Brexit is not the future of Europe".[6]

Capital Markets Union

Unlike American firms, European firms depend in a majority on bank credit. In his 2016 State of the Union Address, Jean-Claude Juncker stated: "An economy almost entirely dependent on bank credit is bad for financial stability. And it is bad for

[3]Christophory, Jul (1984), *Luxembourgeois, qui êtes-vous?: échos et chuchotements*, Chap. 8: *Prospérité, Démographie et Piston*, second edition, Luxembourg, G. Binsfeld, p.135.

[4]Speech *Die europäischen Institutionen*, 15 January 2002, Albin Wallinger and Serge Spellini (2013, *Prominente über Jean-Claude Juncker*, Luxemburg, Prom Verlag, p.115.

[5]Juncker, Jean-Claude, *State of the Union Address 2017*, https://ec.europa.eu/commission/presscorner/detail/en/SPEECH_17_3165

[6]Ibid.

business, as we saw during the financial crisis. That is why it is now urgent we accelerate our work on the capital markets union. The Commission is putting a concrete roadmap for this on your table today”.[7]

Immigration

Jean-Claude Juncker reminded Europeans that, in every family, at least one member was once a refugee: “We Europeans should remember well that Europe is a continent where nearly everyone has at one time been a refugee. Our common history is marked by millions of Europeans fleeing from religious or political persecution, from war, dictatorship, or oppression”.[8]

In his book *Die Rehabilitation des Politischen: von der angeblichen Ohnmacht der Politik vor der nur scheinbaren Allmacht der Wirtschaft*, Romain Kirt explained that: “Luxembourg is inevitably one of the most prosperous countries in the world. Added to this is the fact that we Luxembourgers have a long history of openness to the outside world and diversity within our frontiers; we have always been the paradigm of the open society described by Karl Popper; we have, so to speak, a tradition of openness and diversity. This is why the name Luxembourg is often associated not only with a small, prosperous state in the heart of Europe, but also and above all with a state of mind whose constituent elements are openness, tolerance and hospitality (towards immigrant workers)”.[9]

Jean-Claude Juncker, who was the President of the European Commission from 2014 to 2019, considered that posted workers should enjoy the same rights as other workers within the European Union: “In a Union of equals, there can be no second class workers. Workers should earn the same pay for the same work in the same place”.[10]

---

[7] Juncker, Jean-Claude, *State of the Union Address 2016*, https://op.europa.eu/en/publication-detail/-/publication/c9ff4ff6-9a81-11e6-9bca-01aa75ed71a1/language-en/format-PDF/source-30945725

[8] Juncker, Jean-Claude, *State of the Union Address 2015*, https://commission.europa.eu/system/files/2015-12/state_of_the_union_2015_en.pdf

[9] Romain Kirt, *Die Rehabilitation des Politischen: von der angeblichen Ohnmacht der Politik vor der nur scheinbaren Allmacht der Wirtschaft*, Esch-sur-Alzette, Le Phare, 2002, p.72.

[10] Juncker, Jean-Claude, *State of the Union Address 2017*, https://ec.europa.eu/commission/presscorner/detail/en/SPEECH_17_3165

Tax Havens

In 2008, Jean-Claude Juncker revealed that: "President Sarkozy and Prime Minister François Fillon have assured me that they were not thinking of Luxembourg when they criticised tax havens".[11]

To combat tax evasion, Luxembourg did end up agreeing to abandon its strict bank secrecy laws in the case of European citizens having opened bank accounts in the country. In 2013, Jean-Claude Juncker, then Luxembourg's Prime Minister, told the European Parliament that: "We can, without great damage, introduce automatic exchange of information as of January 1, 2015".[12]

Small Nations

Jean-Claude Juncker had this to say about small countries and what distinguished them from big countries: "Small countries need an intelligent niche policy. Big countries sell arms, small countries sell niches".[13]

In *Mon Luxembourg: un pays à découvrir*, the Franco-Luxembourg historian Stéphane Bern [1963–], who has undoubtedly done more to promote European civilisation than any man of culture before him, wrote: "At the crossroads of Europe, where Latin and Germanic civilisations meet, the Grand Duchy of Luxembourg has always managed to preserve its rich landscapes and sites, combined with industrial and economic success, without ever losing its strong cultural identity even after a long history of foreign occupation. Because of its geographical location, the small size of its territory and the political and economic constraints it faces, Luxembourg has been able to combine its fierce desire for independence with its willingness to play an active part in Europe's construction".[14]

A 2020 article *Qu'est-ce qu'un petit pays*[15] by historian Claude Wey [1954–] explains that: "Luxembourg is certainly a small, multicultural country that is

[11] Luxemburger Wort, 22 October 2008, also Tageblatt 6 June 2008, Wallinger, Albin and Spellini, Serge (2013) *Prominente über Jean-Claude Juncker*, Luxembourg: Prom Verlag, p.97.

[12] https://jp.reuters.com/article/us-luxembourg-banks-idINBRE93908V20130410

[13] RTL Radio Lëtzebuerg, 3 July 2002, Wallinger, Albin and Spellini, Serge (2013) *Prominente über Jean-Claude Juncker*, Luxemburg: Prom Verlag, p.54.

[14] Bern, Stéphane (2016), *Mon Luxembourg : un pays à découvrir*, photographs by de Laubier, Guillaume, Paris, Flammarion, p. 136.

[15] Wey, Claude (2020), *Qu'est-ce qu'un petit pays?, L'économiste Thomas Piketty, l'historien Pascal Ory, l'écrivain Nicolas Mathieu et le Luxembourg,* in the Weekly *Lëtzebuerger Land* of 25 December 2020.

economically rich and politically stable, as well as being a dynamic pole of attraction for the Greater Region.[16] Remarkably endowed materially, this 'small country' is nevertheless struggling to solve the problems of regional planning and road infrastructure, to remedy the widespread housing crisis, to address the failings of the health and hospital services, to promote sustainable economic development and to shed its image as a 'tax haven'".[17]

Globalisation

On the occasion of the conference held on 29 September 2006 about globalisation in the Duchy of Luxembourg, Jean-Claude Juncker asked: "Where is it written, even in the Holy Scriptures, that there is a natural right of Luxembourgers and their neighbours to claim the wealth of the world for themselves alone and exclusively? By the same denying that others have any claim to that prosperity?"[18]

Tax on Financial Transactions

In September 2009, Jean-Claude Juncker explained that: "If one needs a stamp to drive out of a vehicle inspection station, but no tax is paid on financial transactions, then something is wrong. But when I say this, bankers break out in a cold sweat".[19]

Housing

In 2011, Fernand Entringer wrote: "We need to rethink the notion of territory. It's not enough to rant from time to time about property speculation in Luxembourg; we need to tackle the issue intelligently. It can only be tackled in the context of the

[16] The Greater Region is delimited by the rivers Rhine, Saar, Meuse and Moselle. Stretching over some 65,000 square kilometres, it has 11.6 million inhabitants. It encompasses the Lorraine in the French region Grand Est, Wallonia, the Federation Wallonia-Brussels and Ostbelgien in Belgium, Saarland and Rhineland-Palatinate in Germany as well as the Grand Duchy of Luxembourg.
Source: https://www.granderegion.net/en/The-Greater-Region-at-a-Glance

[17] Wey, Claude (2020), *Qu'est-ce qu'un petit pays?, L'économiste Thomas Piketty, l'historien Pascal Ory, l'écrivain Nicolas Mathieu et le Luxembourg,* in the Weekly *Lëtzebuerger Land* of 25 December 2020.

[18] Globalisierung in Luxemburg, conference held on 29 September 2006, Wallinger, Albin and Spellini, Serge (2013) *Prominente über Jean-Claude Juncker*, Luxemburg: Prom Verlag, p. 80.

[19] Télécran, Luxembourg, 23 September 2009, Wallinger, Albin and Spellini, Serge (2013) *Prominente über Jean-Claude Juncker*, Luxemburg: Prom Verlag, p. 19.

Greater Region, which means resolving a number of issues, particularly tax issues".[20]

In the March 2023 article *Éléments de réflexion sur la situation du logement,* the economist Michel-Édouard Ruben provided the following analysis: "80% of Luxembourgers own their main residence - which is comfortably high - and 50% of foreign residents do too - which is almost double the 26% average rate of homeownership for foreign residents in European countries. Luxembourg is therefore what can best be described as a homeowner's democracy".[21]

By comparison, 57.7% of French households own their main residence.

[20] Entringer, Fernand, *Une structure moribonde—Les 25 ans du Centre d'études libérales*, Weekly Lëtzebuerger Land of 5 October 2011, p. 13, https://viewer.eluxemburgensia.lu/ark:70795/b0p6bz/pages/13

[21] Rube, Michel-Édouard, *Éléments de réflexion sur la situation du logement*, Entreprises Magazine, March 2023, Senior Economist, Fondation IDEA asbl, https://www.entreprisesmagazine.com/fr/articles/elements-de-reflexion-sur-la-situation-du-logement

Austria

State

Friedrich von Hayek [1899–1992] was a Nobel Prize winner who clashed publicly with Keynes, criticising his *Treatise on Money*. Hayek denounced the excess of credit due to lax monetary policy, which he said led to crises. He encouraged savings, which reduced the yawning gap between investment and its financing exposed during crises. But it was above all Keynesian policies that he opposed throughout his life. For him, with rare exceptions, state intervention in the economy only made things worse.

Throughout his life, Hayek demonstrated how Keynesian economic stimulus policies based on the use of the public budget produced inflation, stagnation, and unemployment over the long term. Hayek blamed the lengthy inflation experienced post-war on these policies, as well as the rise in unemployment and low growth experienced by Western economies from the 1970s onwards. It was no coincidence that it was in 1974 that Hayek was awarded the Nobel Prize, for by then economic reality had revealed the limitations of the Keynesian theory that Hayek had denounced from the outset in the 1930s.

Economist

Hayek's arguments are not only economic but also sociological, psychological, and political, because as he put it: "But nobody can be a great economist who is only an economist - and I am even tempted to add that the

C. Peicuti, *The European Economy in 100 Quotes*, Contributions to Economics,
https://doi.org/10.1007/978-3-031-68819-5_15

economist who is only an economist is likely to become a nuisance if not a positive danger".[1]

In his speech at the Nobel Banquet, Hayek confessed that: "If I had been consulted whether to establish a Nobel Prize in economics, I should have decidedly advised against it". He added: "The Nobel Prize confers on an individual an authority which in economics no man ought to possess".[2] He argued that this went against the spontaneous order of society that renders it economically efficient.

Competition

In *The Road to Serfdom* published in 1944, Hayek drew an apt comparison between competition and justice: "It is significant that one of the commonest objections to competition is that it is 'blind'. It is not irrelevant to recall that to the ancients blindness was an attribute of their deity of justice. Although competition and justice may have little else in common, it is as much a commendation of competition as of justice that it is no respecter of persons".[3]

The economist added: "In no system that could be rationally defended would the state just do nothing. An effective competitive system needs an intelligently designed and continuously adjusted legal framework as much as any other".[4]

For Hayek, market competition exists because it is imperfect. He equates this to a process of learning and coordinating dispersed, multiple, and incomplete information.

Hayek considered that: "The fact that the opportunities open to the poor in a competitive society are much more restricted than those open to the rich does not make it less true that in such a society the poor are much more free than a person commanding much greater material comfort in a different type of society. Although under competition the probability that a man who starts poor will reach great wealth is much smaller than is true of the man who has inherited property, it is not only possible for the former, but the competitive system is the only one where it depends

---

[1] Hayek, Friedrich A. von (1967), *Studies in Philosophy, Politics and Economics*, Taylor & Francis Books Ltd.

[2] Hayek, Friedrich A. von, speech at the Nobel Banquet, 10 December 1974, NobelPrize.org. Nobel Prize Outreach AB 2023. Fri. 27 Oct 2023. https://www.nobelprize.org/prizes/economic-sciences/1974/hayek/speech/

[3] Hayek, Friedrich A. von (1944), *The Road to Serfdom*, Routledge Press.

[4] Ibid.

solely on him and not on the favours of the mighty, and where nobody can prevent a man from attempting to achieve this result".[5]

He added: "It is only because we have forgotten what unfreedom means that we often overlook the patent fact that in every real sense a badly paid unskilled worker in this country has more freedom to shape his life than many a small entrepreneur in Germany or a much better paid engineer or manager in Russia".[6]

And went on to say: "Whether it is a question of changing his job or the place where he lives, of professing certain views or of spending his leisure in a particular manner, although sometimes the price he may have to pay for following his inclinations may be high, and to many appear too high, there are no absolute impediments, no dangers to bodily security and freedom that confine him by brute force to the task and the environment to which a superior has assigned him".[7]

Economic Sciences

For Hayek: "The curious task of economics is to demonstrate to men how little they really know about what they imagine they can design".[8]

Freedom to Undertake

Hayek believed that economic freedom is the cement of democracy: "The economic freedom which is the prerequisite of any other freedom cannot be the freedom from economic care which the socialists promise us and which can be obtained only by relieving the individual at the same time of the necessity and of the power of choice; it must be the freedom of our economic activity which, with the right of choice, inevitably also carries the risk and the responsibility of that right".[9]

[5] Hayek, Friedrich A. von (1967), *Studies in Philosophy, Politics and Economics*, Taylor & Francis Books Ltd.

[6] Ibid.

[7] Ibid.

[8] Hayek, Friedrich A. von (1991), *The Fatal Conceit: The Errors of Socialism (Volume 1)*, University of Chicago Press; first edition.

[9] Hayek, Friedrich A. von (1944), *The Road to Serfdom*, Routledge Press.

Command or Planned Economy

From the 1930s onwards, Hayek was a staunch adversary of socialist planning. He argued that, as the economy is constantly changing, even the information that is quantifiable will be obsolete by the time it has been processed by the central planner. Furthermore, the information needed is too vast, too complex, and dispersed across society, what has become known as Hayek's 'knowledge problem'. Only the market is capable of capturing and bringing together the fragmented knowledge of the various members of society and doing the work of the planner in real time. Hayek developed the 'theory of spontaneous orders', which are not the result of a deliberate plan, but of uncoordinated actions. According to his theory, market equilibrium is a spontaneous order.

History would prove that Hayek was right when he asserted in 1944 that a state that ran a country's economy was bound to tear down individual freedoms. His view was that a command economy leads to totalitarianism and that only the market economy is compatible with democracy: "When it becomes dominated by a collectivist creed, democracy will inevitably destroy itself".[10]

He warned that: "While there is nothing in modern technological developments which forces us towards comprehensive economic planning, there is a great deal in them which makes infinitely more dangerous the power a planning authority would possess".[11]

And pointed out that: "It would make the very men who are most anxious to plan society the most dangerous if they were allowed to do so - and the most intolerant of the planning of others".[12]

Demarchy

For Hayek, democracy is a means, not an end in itself: "Democracy is essentially a means, a utilitarian device for safeguarding internal peace and individual freedom".[13]

Democracy must submit to a body of formulated laws. If the scope of the State's action is not limited, the population may constantly push for more and more expenditure, which could eventually threaten the market order. Hayek resurrected

[10] Ibid.
[11] Ibid.
[12] Ibid.
[13] Ibid.

the archaic term 'demarchy'[14] to describe such a state of affairs, explaining that: "Unless we restore a situation in which governments (and other public authorities) find that if they overspend they will, like everybody else, be unable to meet their obligations, there will be no halt to this growth which, by substituting collective for private activity, threatens to suffocate individual initiative. Under the prevailing form of unlimited democracy, in which government has power to confer special material benefits on groups, it is forced to buy the support of sufficient numbers to add up to a majority".[15]

Money

Hayek considered that: "Money is one of the greatest instruments of freedom ever invented by man".[16]

Pioneering endocrinologist Hans Selye [1907–1982], who was nominated 17 times but never won the Nobel Prize in Physiology or Medicine, and who coined the term stress and conceptualized its physiology, considered that: "For example, money cannot be the ultimate goal; it has no value in itself. It can only serve as a means to an end that is valuable to us in its own right".

Phillips Curve

In an article published in 1958, the economist Alban Phillips [1914–1975] explained, by means of a curve that would bear his name, that he had observed an inverse relationship between money wage changes and unemployment in the British economy. Until the first oil shock, this economic theory greatly influenced Keynesian policies, which Hayek criticised throughout his life, explaining that: "Since it has become generally understood that whoever controls the total supply of money of a country has thereby power to give in most situations almost instantaneous relief to unemployment, even if only at the price of much unemployment later, the political pressure on such an agency must become irresistible".[17]

---

[14] Hayek, Friedrich A. von (1993), *Law, Legislation and Liberty*, Routledge Press.

[15] Hayek, Friedrich A. von (1999), from *Good Money, Part II Volume Six of the Collected Works of F.A. Hayek*, edited by Stephen Kresge, Routledge.

[16] Hayek, Friedrich A. von (1944), *The Road to Serfdom*, Routledge Press.

[17] Hayek, Friedrich A. von (1990), *Denationalisation of Money - The Argument Refined, An Analysis of the Theory and Practice of Concurrent Currencies*, The Institute of Economic Affairs.

Institutions

Hayek invited his contemporaries to reflect on the institutional mechanisms that led to Nazism: "The contention that only the peculiar wickedness of the Germans has produced the Nazi system is likely to become the excuse for forcing on us the very institutions which have produced that wickedness".[18]

Liberalism

Hayek defined liberalism thus: "There is nothing in the basic principles of liberalism to make it a stationary creed, there are no hard-and-fast rules fixed once and for all. The fundamental principle that in the ordering of our affairs, we should make as much use as possible of the spontaneous forces of society, and resort as little as possible to coercion, is capable of an infinite variety of applications".[19]

Socialism

In 1943, in *The Road to Serfdom*, Friedrich von Hayek warned that the transition of Western societies to socialism was not natural: "How sharp a break not only with the recent past but with the whole evolution of Western civilisation the modern trend towards socialism means, becomes clear if we consider it not merely against the background of the nineteenth century, but in a longer historical perspective. We are rapidly abandoning not the views merely of Cobden and Bright, of Adam Smith and Hume, or even of Locke and Milton, but one of the salient characteristics of Western civilisation as it has grown from the foundations laid by Christianity and the Greeks and Romans. Not merely nineteenth- and eighteenth-century liberalism, but the basic individualism inherited by us from Erasmus and Montaigne, from Cicero and Tacitus, Pericles and Thucydides is progressively relinquished".[20]

---

[18] Hayek, Friedrich A. von (1944), *The Road to Serfdom*, Routledge Press.

[19] Ibid.

[20] Ibid.

Croatia

Work

According to writer and politician Ante Starčević [1823–1896]: "Clean work does not fear the light".

Money

Musician, writer, actor, painter, poet, and aphorist Toma Bebić [1935–1990] confessed that: "All my life, I made the mistake of thinking that there were other ideals in life than money".

The writer Ante Kovačić [1854–1889] concluded: "After all, money is money. The biggest, strongest and most perfect master in the world".

Competition

The satirist Pajo Kanižaj [1939–]: "A man fights while he's young that the young may never have to fight in their turn."

Gifts

The novelist and playwright Mirko Božić [1919–1995] warned that the image we project when we make a gift is more that of a vassal than a master: "Giving can humble a person".

C. Peicuti, *The European Economy in 100 Quotes*, Contributions to Economics,
https://doi.org/10.1007/978-3-031-68819-5_16

Wealth

The poet and playwright Marin Držić [1508–1567] considered that: “Kindness is drowned out by gold”.

Ante Starčević drew attention to the abyssal inequalities in our society, writing: “One person can spend more than millions of people can save”.

Benedikt Kotruljević [1400–1468], who was born in Ragusa (modern-day Dubrovnik) and served as a diplomat of the Kingdom of Naples, had these words of advice: “If you want to be rich, work hard and buy sparingly”.

Public Debt

Novelist and short-story writer Ivan Raos [1921–1987] explained why the public is not outraged by the growing public debt as follows: “When financed out of the state coffers, it is not a heartache, not even for the stingiest of misers”.

Human Resources

As explained by Toma Bebić: “When a boss talks about his staff, it’s criticism; and when they talk about him, it’s gossip”.

On the loneliness of leadership, Toma Bebić had this to say: “A lion generally lives alone, jackals in a community”.

Aid

The essayist, poet, and novelist Vladimir Nazor [1876–1949] observed: “I don’t know where it comes from, but almost all the people you help cease to be your friends”.

According to the writer Ante Dukić [1867–1952]: “The poor help the poor in the sincerest way”.

Work

For Ante Dukić: "Work and order are twins".

He explained non-stop work in this way: "As he works non-stop, he is never tired after work".

Poor

Toma Bebić believed that: "Great deeds are generally accomplished by people of modest means".

Idleness

Ante Dukić considered that: "The devil does his best business with the idle".

Sweden

Economic Cycle and Taxation

In 1974, Gunnar Myrdal [1898–1987] and Friedrich von Hayek shared the Sveriges Riksbank Prize in Economic Sciences in Memory of Alfred Nobel "for their pioneering work in the theory of money and economic fluctuations and for their penetrating analysis of the interdependence of economic, social and institutional phenomena".[1]

A statesman, Gunnar Myrdal helped improve Sweden's budget and proposed the introduction of a new fiscal paradigm compatible with a reasoned use of the deficit. As he explained in 1939: "The chief technical problem of fiscal policy in the business cycle is, therefore, to design formulas for public finance which, as part of the regular system, make room for deficit spending during depressions by securing the building up of corresponding surpluses in good years".[2]

Economy

For Gunnar Myrdal, economics is the most political of the sciences. Economic knowledge is not derived from empirical research, but from what questions are asked. He highlighted the ideological basis of contemporary economic theory, the fact that all research is preceded by an initial choice of values on which the theoretical discourse is based. He invited economists to make explicit the values on which their theories are based.

---

[1] https://www.nobelprize.org/prizes/economic-sciences/1974/myrdal/facts/

[2] Myrdal, Gunnar (1939), *Fiscal Policy in the Business Cycle*, from Readings in Fiscal Policy, American Economic Association (1955).

C. Peicuti, *The European Economy in 100 Quotes*, Contributions to Economics,
https://doi.org/10.1007/978-3-031-68819-5_17

His view is that the development of economic theory is a response to the dominant interests of the moment. Thus, without the crisis of 1929, there would have been no Keynesian heyday.

As he put it: "I am often considered almost not a part of the profession of Establishment economists. I am even referred to as a sociologist. And by that, economists usually do not mean anything flattering".

Poverty

Gunnar Myrdal considered that poverty breeds poverty and that laissez-faire does not contribute to rebalancing but to reinforcing inequalities. He developed the theory of circular cumulative causation. In the vicious circle that is poverty, the delinquency rate and inadequate education have a significant impact on the level of unemployment and wages. Inequalities, often seen as a source of cheap labour and capital accumulation for the rich, are in fact a brake on a country's economic development. Low wages reduce demand and the nation deprives itself of the talent of the poorest, which would help it outperform in the global economic war.

In 1944, two decades before the Civil Rights Movement, Gunnar Myrdal published *An American Dilemma: The Negro Problem and Modern Democracy*, a study of race relations providing historic, economic, and sociological insights. The author denounced racism in the United States, responsible for the poverty and cultural marginalisation of the negro community. He explained that: "To the great majority of white Americans, the Negro problem has distinctly negative connotations. It suggests something difficult to settle and equally difficult to leave alone. It is embarrassing. It makes for moral uneasiness".[3]

This book played a decisive role in the US Supreme Court's unanimous ruling in 1954 that racial segregation in public schools violated the Fourteenth Amendment to the Constitution.

Nevertheless, Gunnar Myrdal considered that: "Compared with members of other nations of Western civilization, the ordinary American is a rationalistic being, and there are close relations between his moralism and his rationalism. Even romanticism, transcendentalism, and mysticism tend to be, in the American culture, rational, pragmatic and optimistic".[4] His view was that: "The ordinary American is the opposite of a cynic. He is on the average more of a believer and a defender of the

[3]Myrdal, Gunnar (1944), with the assistance of Sterner, Richard, and Rose, Arnold, *An American Dilemma: The Negro Problem and Modern Democracy*, Harper and Brothers Publishers.
[4]Ibid.

faith in humanity than the rest of the Occidentals. It is a relatively important matter to him to be true to his own ideals and to carry them out in actual life".[5]

Inequalities

In *Economic Theory and Under-Developed Regions* published in 1959, Myrdal wrote: "The purpose of economic development is to raise levels of living for the masses of the people".

He went on: "[. . .] in a progressive society [. . .] the improvement of the lot of the poor can often be won without substantial sacrifices from those who are better off and is sometimes not only compatible with, but a condition for, the attainment of higher levels in all income brackets, including the higher ones".

Myrdal drew attention to the fact that: "There is a tendency inherent in the free play of market forces to create regional inequalities, and that this tendency becomes the more dominant the poorer a country is, are two of the most important laws of economic underdevelopment and development under laissez-faire".[6]

Comparative Advantage

Comparative advantage occurs when a country can produce a particular type of good at a lower opportunity cost than another country. As David Ricardo [1772–1823] explained in 1817, comparative advantage is a powerful argument in favour of free trade.

In 1977, Bertil Ohlin [1899–1979] and British economist James Meade [1907–1997] shared the Sveriges Riksbank Prize in Economic Sciences in Memory of Alfred Nobel "for their pathbreaking contribution to the theory of international trade and international capital movements". Bertil Ohlin was the leader of the People's Party, a social-liberal party, from 1944 to 1967, served briefly as the country's Minister of Commerce and Industry from 1944 to 1945 and chaired the Economic Sciences Prize Committee at the Royal Swedish Academy of Sciences from 1969 to 1974.

---

[5]Ibid.

[6]Myrdal, Gunnar (1957), *Economic Theory and Under-Developed Regions*, reprinted 1964, University Paperbacks, Methuen & Co. Ltd.

Bertil Ohlin sought to understand the origin of comparative advantage. He explained inter-regional and international trade in terms of the relative abundance or scarcity of the various factors of production with which different countries are endowed, what became known as the factor-endowments approach. Each country has an interest in specialising in the factors of production that it possesses in abundance relative to other countries, exporting goods that contain these abundant factors and importing goods that require factors that it possesses in smaller quantities or that it lacks. Bertil Ohlin thereby demonstrated the benefits of specialisation and free trade. This is how he explained North-South relations. Since the countries of the North are more richly endowed in capital (plant, equipment, technology) than the countries of the South, they specialise in capital-intensive products with high added value. Conversely, countries in the South with more labour than capital specialise in labour-intensive goods with low added value, such as clothing. This became known as the Heckscher-Ohlin theorem. Eli Heckscher [1879–1952] was credited as co-developer. Many ideas in the final model came from Ohlin's doctoral thesis that was supervised by Heckscher, who in 1919 had already provided a model explaining patterns in international trade,[7] arguing that trade was not determined by technological differences, but by different quantities or endowments of factors of production.

Public Debt

When Bertil Ohlin sent extracts of his thesis to the *Economic Journal* for publication, it was turned down by the then editor John Maynard Keynes, who returned the manuscript with a blunt rejection note: "This amounts to nothing and should be refused. J.M. Keynes".[8] This was the start of a long series of controversies. Bertil Ohlin even criticised Keynes in his Nobel Memorial Lecture for an excessively static approach to expectations.

Bertil Ohlin can be considered a precursor of Keynes in that, as early as 1927, he advocated an expansionary fiscal policy. He argued that public debt could be repaid when the economy recovered because the more people were in work, the greater would be the demand for goods.

---

[7]Heckscher, Eli (1919), *The Effect of Foreign Trade on the Distribution of Income*, Ekonomisk Tidskrift, 497–512. Reprinted as Chap. 13 in A.E.A. (1949). Readings in the Theory of International Trade, 272-300 (Philadelphia: Blakiston) with a Translation in H. Flam and M. J. Flanders (Eds.). 1991. Heckscher-Ohlin Trade Theory, 43-69. Cambridge: MIT Press.

[8]Gans, Joshua and Shepherd, George (1994), *How Are the Mighty Fallen: Rejected Classic Articles by Leading Economists*, The Journal of Economic Perspectives, Vol. 8, No. 1 (Winter, 1994), pp. 165-179.

International Trade

Bertil Ohlin argued that: "The international trade theory has, in my opinion, given far too much attention to the effects of certain variations, for example, in duties, on the national incomes, and too little to the effects on individual incomes. [...] In many cases, changes in the sums count for very little, while changes in the individual incomes are distinctly relevant".[9]

The pharaonic reparations demanded of Germany after the First World War led to much debate. When France was vanquished in the Napoleonic Wars, it did not lose much at the Congress of Vienna and was able to get back on its feet. Not so Germany, which was driven into a corner. This would lead to the Second World War.

The *Water Lilies Cycle*[10] was offered to the French State by painter Claude Monet on the day after the Armistice of 11 November 1918 as a symbol of peace; the paintings were installed at the Orangerie Museum in 1927, a few months after his death. For there to have been a lasting peace, a good peace treaty would have been needed...

In 1929, Ohlin and Keynes clashed over the question of whether Germany was able to make the war reparation payments imposed by the Treaty of Versailles. The controversy was over the transfer problem. Though the payment of war reparations represented a transfer of buying power to the victors, Ohlin's view was that Germany would get by through exports that these countries would buy. He contended that to be able to export its products, Germany would not even have to lower their prices. Keynes considered that unless German exports were favoured, there was no guarantee that the countries in receipt of war reparations would buy German products.

Greenhouse Effect

In the chapter on the emergence of a climate conscience in his book *Le climat après la fin du mois*, Christian Gollier explained that: "Although France's Joseph Fourier put forward this idea seven decades earlier, it is generally accepted that it was the Swedish chemist Svante August Arrhenius [1859–1927], the winner of the Nobel Prize for Chemistry in 1903, who scientifically constructed the hypothesis of a greenhouse effect produced by CO_2 in the atmosphere. In 1896, he published an

[9] Ohlin, Berthil (1935), *Interregional and International Trade*, Harvard Economic Studies.
[10] *Cycle des Nymphéas.*

article entitled *On the Influence of Carbonic Acid*[11] *in the Air upon the Temperature of the Ground,*[12] which contains a theory to explain the glacial cycles experienced by the Earth by reference to variations in the concentration of CO_2 in the atmosphere".[13]

Climate Science

Arrhenius went further and laid the foundation for climate science, which states that global warming occurs because human activity increases the concentration of greenhouse gases in the atmosphere. This is not a marginal change, but a radical change compared with typical temperatures over the last 10,000 years. "He estimated that a doubling of this concentration [CO_2] would increase the average temperature by around five degrees Celsius. He believed that at the rate at which the West was burning coal to produce the energy needed for its Industrial Revolution, it would take three millennia for this doubling to occur. He understood that this greenhouse gas was why the Earth enjoyed a temperate climate in its time".[14]

Arrhenius did not foresee the extent to which the Industrial Revolution and globalisation would lead to exponential growth in emissions, accelerating global warming. In the Headline Statements drawn from the Synthesis Report of the Sixth Assessment Report published in March 2023 by the Intergovernmental Panel on Climate Change,[15] the Group of Experts concluded that "continued greenhouse gas emissions will lead to increasing global warming, with the best estimate of reaching 1.5 °C in the near term in considered scenarios and modelled pathways".[16] In their views, "cumulative carbon emissions until the time of reaching net-zero CO_2 emissions and the level of greenhouse gas emission reductions this decade largely determine whether warming can be limited to 1.5 °C or 2 °C".[17]

[11] Throughout this paper, Arrhenius refers to carbon dioxide as "carbonic acid" in accordance with the convention at the time he was writing.

[12] https://www.rsc.org/images/Arrhenius1896_tcm18-173546.pdf

[13] Gollier, Christian (2019), *Le climat après la fin du mois*, Edition PUF, p.21.

[14] Ibid.

[15] Summary for Policymakers IPCC, 2023: Summary for Policymakers. In: Climate Change 2023: Synthesis Report. Contribution of Working Groups I, II and III to the Sixth Assessment Report of the Intergovernmental Panel on Climate Change [Core Writing Team, H. Lee and J. Romero (eds.)]. IPCC, Geneva, Switzerland, pp. 1-34, doi: 10.59327/IPCC/AR6-9789291691647.001.

[16] Ibid.

[17] Ibid.

Central Bank

Chronologically the oldest central bank in Europe is Rikets Ständers Bank (which would later change its name to Riksbank), which was founded in 1688 in Stockholm to issue "real" banknotes.

Cyprus

Unemployment

The 2010 Sveriges Riksbank Prize in Economic Sciences in Memory of Alfred Nobel was awarded to Cypriot economist Christopher Pissarides [1948–] and American economists Peter Diamond [1940–] and Dale Mortensen [1939–2014] "for their analysis of markets with search frictions".[1] According to the press release by the Royal Swedish Academy of Sciences, the three laureates demonstrated that "more generous unemployment benefits give rise to higher unemployment and longer search times." The subject of the Prize Lecture by Christopher Pissarides was "Equilibrium in the Labour Market with Search Frictions".[2]

Peter Diamond and Dale Mortensen did draw attention to the fact that unemployment benefits are not permanent. In most countries, they are received for a limited duration. The economists also showed that unemployment insurance gives the unemployed time to find a job that best matches their skills. This is beneficial to the economy as a whole: if overqualified people take jobs that are below their skills, those who have the profile for those jobs will no longer be able to access them. Unemployment insurance is therefore good for economic efficiency. However, if unemployment benefits match wages, this can act as a disincentive.

Why are so many people unemployed at the same time that there are a large number of job openings? For the three laureates, the answer is simple: in any market, it takes time to match supply and demand. There is no such thing as immediacy (this also applies to the property market, for example). Given the heterogeneity of supply, it takes time and resources to identify the right job (or the right property). Other non-market factors can lengthen the time taken: slow job creation due to the

[1] https://www.nobelprize.org/uploads/2018/06/press-12.pdf

[2] https://www.nobelprize.org/prizes/economic-sciences/2010/pissarides/lecture/

C. Peicuti, *The European Economy in 100 Quotes*, Contributions to Economics,
https://doi.org/10.1007/978-3-031-68819-5_18

economic cycle, growth, or a gradual exit from the crisis (just as in the case of property, a rise in interest rates can limit access to credit and thus lengthen the time taken to sell before property prices adjust and fall). By its very nature, the labour market is frictional (as is the property market).

Christopher Pissarides and Dale Mortensen systematically developed and applied the theory proposed by Peter Diamond in a model that became known as the Diamond-Mortensen-Pissarides (DMP) model. This deals with markets with search friction, in which the cost, time, and effort spent by economic agents on searching and matching are central. The main assumption is that players behave rationally. The two economists reached two paradoxical conclusions regarding unemployment: it is a factor of equilibrium and it is an efficient vehicle to move workers from one productive activity to another, which would be considerably harder if there was full employment, contributing to a better functioning of the economy.

Finland

Contracts

Bengt Holmström [1949–] shared the 2016 Sveriges Riksbank Prize in Economic Sciences in Memory of Alfred Nobel with British economist Oliver Hart [1948–] "for their contributions to contract theory".[1]

Holmström's pioneering research in the 1970s demonstrated that, for a contract to be optimal from the point of view of the employer or shareholders, it must take account of "asymmetric information", "uncertainties", and "divergent interests".

CEO Remuneration

In his Prize Lecture, Pay for Performance and Beyond, delivered in 2016, Holmström declared: "Today, I know better. As I will try to explain, one of the main lessons from working on incentive problems for 25 years is, that within firms, high-powered financial incentives can be very dysfunctional and attempts to bring the market inside the firm are generally misguided. Typically, it is best to avoid high-powered incentives and sometimes not use pay-for-performance at all".[2]

Holmström was sceptical about the economic efficiency of basing the chief executive officer's remuneration on share price performance. He believed that this remuneration should be indexed at least to the company's share price relative to that of other companies in the same sector.

[1] https://www.nobelprize.org/prizes/economic-sciences/2016/summary/

[2] Holmström, Bengt (2016), Pay For Performance and Beyond, Prize Lecture, 8 December 2016, https://www.nobelprize.org/uploads/2018/06/holmstrom-lecture.pdf

C. Peicuti, *The European Economy in 100 Quotes*, Contributions to Economics,
https://doi.org/10.1007/978-3-031-68819-5_19

For example, if indexed solely to the company's performance, the chief executive officer of an oil company would earn a higher remuneration simply because the price of oil has increased. Yet that is out of his control, and there is therefore no reason why he should be rewarded.

Stock Options

Stock options give the holder the right, but not the obligation, to buy stock at an agreed-upon price and date. Employee stock options are a type of compensation given by a company to some employees or executives to buy stock at a preferential price that has been agreed upon.

The rise in the price of the underlying shares guarantees a very high return for the stock option holders in the sureness of time. Yet, very often, they played no part in the rise in the share price. What's more, in many countries, the tax treatment of stock options is very advantageous.

Holmström advised against a system of stock options for not being demanding enough on the beneficiaries and because there is a near-certain payoff since share prices often appreciate for reasons to do with the economy and/or the sector.

One might add that, as the liquidity in circulation has continued to increase globally as a result of monetary policies and economic support measures during the COVID-19 pandemic, and as the number of assets has remained limited by nature, the rise in share prices is likely to be such that, almost automatically, stock options will be in the money, that is above their exercise price.

Enterprise

Holmström considered the firm as an "incentive system" whose objective is to ensure a maximum effort by employees by combining authority, ownership and pay-for-performance.

Bonuses

Part of Holmström's research was devoted to bonuses. He highlighted the difficulty of evaluating employees such as teachers or police officers who perform multiple tasks that are difficult to assess. A poorly calibrated contractual incentive system can have deleterious effects and push these employees to abandon some of the essential duties provided to society in order to focus solely on tasks rewarded with a bonus (what has been described as the folly of hoping for A, while paying for B).

Holmström studied the problems of moral hazard and principal–agent relationship in businesses with regard to bonuses. The principal's problem is to avoid opportunistic behaviour and to design a contract that will provide the right incentives for the agent to act in the principal's interest.

Subordination Relationship

The French Labour Code[3] defines the relationship of subordination as follows: "Irrespective of the type of employment contract, a relationship by which the employer exercises his power of direction over the employee: power to give orders, to monitor their execution and to penalise poor execution of said orders".[4]

Holmström and Hart, the two laureates of the 2016 Sveriges Riksbank Prize in Economic Sciences in Memory of Alfred Nobel, considered that an employment contract need not establish a superior-subordinate relationship if the employer and employee wish to protect their respective investments, the employer seeking to invest in the physical capital, the employee in the specific human capital he embodies.

[3] Code du travail.

[4] https://code.travail.gouv.fr/glossaire/lien-de-subordination

Netherlands

Human Enterprise

Erasmus [1466–1535], also known as Erasmus of Rotterdam, believed that it is through education that we become men: *Fit homo, non nascitur* ("Man is not born, but made man").

Econometrics

The Netherlands has had three Nobel laureates in the field of economic sciences: Jan Tinbergen [1903–1994] in 1969 for his important contributions to econometrics, Tjalling Koopmans [1910–1985] in 1975 for his work on operations research, and Guido Imbens [1963–] in 2021 for new insights about the labour market. The three Dutch Nobel laureates devised new methodologies that revolutionised economic sciences.

Jan Tinbergen created the first aggregate-level macroeconomic model. In 1936, he built a 24-equation econometric model of the Dutch economy to observe which parameters had to be influenced to achieve full employment. He had a go modelling what later would become known as the Phillips curve. His 1939 book, *Business Cycles in the United States, 1919–1932*, included a 48-equation model of the American economy.

In the introduction to his lecture to the memory of Alfred Nobel given in 1969, entitled *The Use of Models: Experience and Prospects*, Jan Tinbergen explained: "The advantages of models are, on one hand, that they force us to present a 'complete' theory by which I mean a theory taking into account all relevant

C. Peicuti, *The European Economy in 100 Quotes*, Contributions to Economics,
https://doi.org/10.1007/978-3-031-68819-5_20

phenomena and relations and, on the other hand, the confrontation with observation, that is, reality. Of course these remarks are far from new".[1]

Going on to say: "Models constitute a framework or a skeleton and the flesh and blood will have to be added by a lot of common sense and knowledge of details".[2]

These dynamic models would become the basis for political decisions and financial forecasts.

In a 1951 article in *Econometrica*, Tinbergen explained: "Econometrics is the name for a field of science in which mathematical-economic and mathematical-statistical research are applied in combination. Econometrics, therefore, forms a borderland between two branches of science, with the advantages and disadvantages thereof; advantages, because new combinations are introduced which often open up new perspectives; disadvantages, because the work in this field requires skill in two domains, which either takes up too much time or leads to insufficient training of its students in one of the two respects".[3]

Coherence Rule

The coherence rule developed by Jan Tinbergen states that policymakers (the State) ideally need as many instruments (fiscal deficit, money supply etc.) as objectives (growth, full employment, price stability etc.).[4]

Welfare State

For objectives in terms of social and individual well-being—such as full employment, reduced inequalities, price stability, and growth—to be achieved in a market economy, Jan Tinbergen considered that a high level of public intervention was required, through a strong public sector, planning, public investment, and

---

[1] Tinbergen, Jan (1969), *The Use of Models: Experience and Prospects*, Prize Lecture. NobelPrize.org. Nobel Prize Outreach AB 2023. Sun. 29 Oct 2023. https://www.nobelprize.org/prizes/economic-sciences/1969/tinbergen/lecture/

Also, Tinbergen, Jan (1981), The Use of Models: Experience and Prospects, American Economic Review, American Economic Association, vol. 71(6), pages 17–22, Special I.

[2] Ibid.

[3] Tinbergen, Jan (1952), Journal of the Staple Inn Actuarial Society, Volume 11, Issue 1, March 1952, pp. 49–5, DOI: https://doi.org/10.1017/S0020269X00004862

[4] Tinbergen, Jan (1952), On *the Theory of Economic Policy*, North-Holland Publishing Company, Amsterdam.

redistributive taxation. The Dutch economist would go down as one of the first theorists of the post-war welfare state.

He considered that: "Educational policies deserve to be programmed not only with a view to improving education in the widest sense, but also in order to influence the income distribution".[5]

Optimum Allocation of Resources

In his biographical, Tjalling Koopmans recalled how he attended lectures by Jan Tinbergen and had the privilege of almost weekly private tutoring over lunch afterwards.

As a result of his work as a statistician for the British Merchant Shipping Mission in Washington during the war, Koopmans, then 32, was asked by the Combined Shipping Adjustment Board to produce a report on the optimal routing and associated costs of transportation on the various routes to England, expressed in ship days, and explaining what he termed the "paradoxes of shipping."

Following this practical experience, Koopmans devoted his academic research to the optimum allocation of resources. He used the technique of linear programming to determine for which goods and services scarce factors such as capital or labour should be used in order to achieve maximum satisfaction of human needs.

Endogenous and Exogenous Shocks

Koopmans was one of the first economists to stress the need to distinguish between endogenous shocks coming from within the economic system (as in the case of the subprimes) and exogenous shocks coming from outside (caused by pandemics and wars).

Economist

Koopmans explained that: "While it was long possible and sometimes tempting for physicists to deny the usefulness of the molecular hypothesis, we economists have the good luck of being some of the 'molecules' of economic life ourselves, and of

[5]Tinbergen, Jan (1975), *Income Distribution: Analysis and Policies*, North-Holland Publishing Company.

having the possibility through human contacts to study the behavior of other 'molecules'".[6]

Economic Theory

Koopmans stated: "We look upon economic theory as a sequence of conceptual models that seek to express in simplified form different aspects of an always more complicated reality".[7]

Experimental Economics

The 2021 Sveriges Riksbank Prize in Economic Sciences in Memory of Alfred Nobel was divided, one half awarded to David Card [1956–] "for his empirical contributions to labour economics", the other half jointly to Joshua Angrist [1960–] and Guido Imbens [1963–] "for their methodological contributions to the analysis of causal relationships",[8] the three laureates have provided new insights about the labour market and shown what conclusions about cause and effect can be drawn from natural experiments, that is conducted in real-life situations. Guido Imbens has argued the social sciences deal more with cause and effect than correlations because this is more useful to policymakers who want to know what will be the effects of certain measures.

Universal Basic Income

Universal basic income refers to a social welfare system in which all citizens of a given country regularly receive guaranteed income in the form of an unconditional transfer payment to meet their basic needs.

Guido Imbens studied the effect of unearned income (gaming, lottery, universal basic income, social transfers) on the labour supply and concluded that it had little effect. In particular, he gathered empirical evidence from a survey of lottery winners in the State of Massachusetts. What he found was while there was some effect on labour supply, lottery winnings did not change how much people worked. After

[6]Koopmans, Tjalling (1957), *Three Essays Three Essays on the State of Economic Science*, McGraw-Hill Book Company, Inc.

[7]Ibid.

[8]https://www.nobelprize.org/prizes/economic-sciences/2021/imbens/facts/

analysing the causal relationship between labour supply and universal income beneficiaries, the Nobel Prize winner demonstrated that when universal basic income is provided, this has a very modest impact on labour supply.

Deficits

In 2002, Willem Frederik Duisenberg (1935–2005), the first President of the European Central Bank from 1998 to 2003, declared: "It is important to remember that the main reason why these countries are experiencing fiscal difficulties is that they failed to take advantage of the strong growth to substantially improve their fiscal situation".

Belgium

Gold

In *Villes tentaculaires*, a collection of 20 poems published in 1920, Émile Verhaeren had this to say:

> The stock exchange
> Like a torso of stone and metal, tall and straight
> The monument of gold in the darkness shakes.
> As soon as night passes and daybreak unfurls,
> The immense crossroads red as pearls
> Where are exalted its daily flutters
> Shudders.

He goes on to describe the activity of banks:

> Banks open early and their counters,
> Where gold is weighed by the tellers,
> See bills of exchange and bank notes,
> Light as leaves, arrive in heaps,
> A fury rises and heads
> To the street and spreads,
> Stoking, from balcony to balcony
> In the city, fear, madness and vanity.

He concluded:

> Like a torso of stone and metal tall and straight,
> Within in its foul mystery curled,
> The beating, gasping heart of the world,
> The monument of gold, in the darkness, shakes.

C. Peicuti, *The European Economy in 100 Quotes*, Contributions to Economics,
https://doi.org/10.1007/978-3-031-68819-5_21

Adversary

Having sizeable adversaries keeps businesses on their toes. Businesses operating in the same sector often take their cue from their rivals, cases in point being Airbus and Boeing in the aeronautics industry, and Kering and LVMH in the luxury sector in their early days. As pointed out by Belgian novelist Amélie Nothomb [1966–] in *Le sabotage amoureux*: "No one on this earth is indispensable, except the enemy".

Sister Emmanuelle [1908–2008] founded Association Sœur Emmanuelle (Asmae), an officially recognised independent, and secular non-profit organisation, known worldwide for its actions to protect and educate the most vulnerable children. An avid reader, the Religious Sister in the Congregation of Our Lady of Sion stated: "I've only been searching for the Absolute for seventy years, and even now I sometimes prefer to read a really good book rather than go and pray!" She believed that: "Pascal was right when he recommended taking at least some steps with your adversary before opposing him".

Sister Emmanuelle explained: "I applied to myself this maxim by Marcus Aurelius, which I often cite to my pupils: 'The impediment to action advances action'".

The religious sister wrote: "The victor, said Napoleon, is the one who lasts an hour longer. Well, you have to fight. You have to hold out one hour longer".

Brand Image

The image of the Parisian woman, established as a world symbol by the 1900 Universal Exhibition in Paris, as evidenced by the medal *La Parisienne* by medallist Jean-Baptiste Émile Dropsy that can be admired at the Musée Carnavalet, will endure according to Amélie Nothomb: "The Parisian woman is legendary: she exists more than the other women, and that for eternity".

France's image is inseparable from that of champagne. As a connoisseur and lover of champagne and of France, Amélie Nothomb defines it as follows in *Pétronille*: "France is this magical country where the most ordinary of bars can serve you anytime a great champagne at the ideal temperature".

Inequalities

In *Péplum*, Amélie Nothomb wrote: "The North-South axis, it is the wealth-poverty axis. The East-West axis is less fundamental: it opposed two cultures, two philosophies. A dialogue seems possible and confrontation is prickly. The North-South axis grabs you at the throat".

Sister Emmanuelle asked herself: "Whence does the well-being of the Cairo rag-picker come from? Whence does the ill-being of Europe's rich come from?"

The religious sister wrote: "This joy in the midst of such destitution is astonishing! Where therefore does man find his happiness? I would ask myself the same question later in Europe, where I was often confronted by a climate of gloom, a fundamental dissatisfaction. I get the impression that people are entangled in a different kind of slavery: desires that are impossible to control, constantly revived, a breathless race with no respite, smothering the slightest pleasure of living, of living in the moment".

She added: "The mystery of the human heart: the most affluent always demand more, our financiers lose sleep; the most destitute make do with their hovels, cobblers and rag-pickers sing".

Sister Emmanuelle exclaimed: "Misery is not measured on the Richter scale like earthquakes!"

Sister Emmanuelle said: "What interests me is justice. Justice requires sharing. [...] Sharing doesn't just mean giving alms, it means distributing the world's wealth fairly. Everyone agrees on the principle, but who is prepared to change their consumption habits?" She added: "I love the poor, not poverty".

Her only hope of there being social justice is for it to be embodied by young people: "I'm speaking to you, young people of France and Europe. Listen to the old woman that I am: born in 1908, I have lived through the most incredible century ever. I have been called to five continents to respond to the tragedies wreaked by poverty, violence and war, everywhere man is a wolf to man. You are the son of your century, you are immersed in everything that is bubbling up around you. I would like to say this to each and every one: be the man or woman you are. If depression is about to knock you down, know this: the strength is in you, in your body and in your heart. Let your thirst for justice carry you towards those less fortunate than you, and join the battle. Believe in yourself, in your passion for a world where free people live as equals, as brothers. Believe in your dynamism; embody your ideal in the very place where you live, where you feel your heart beating. Know that your determination, despite setbacks, will bring triumph. Believe in others: the same breath of justice courses through them. Don't be afraid to join their fight: the union of the young is a formidable power. Believe in yourself, as I believe in you; believe in others as I believe in you!"

Predictions

Predicting the future has always proved impossible and, as Amélie Nothomb wrote in *Péplum*: "To claim to have been exhaustive about the future's potentialities is to set new heights of foolishness".

Degrowth

According to Christian Gollier: "Our collective project should be selective degrowth, leaving people free to express their entrepreneurial genius in activities that are compatible with the common good, while encouraging a reduction in activities that destroy nature".

Overconsumption in developed countries has destroyed the planet. Sister Emmanuelle invites us to stop placing material things at the centre of our existence: "Let us neither be fascinated by the glitter of things", she said, "nor despair at their nothingness. It is possible to rise infinitely above them. Pascal teaches us that there is, oh so very much, a third way. If we hitch our plough to a star, it will take off and pluck us out of nothingness".

Energy Transition

For Christian Gollier: "For a long time now, people have been deceived into thinking that the energy transition is a fantastic opportunity that will make us all richer, create jobs, reduce energy bills and give us back our energy independence from the Gulf States. The reality is quite different. Whether it is a carbon tax, tradable emission permits, vehicle emission standards or thermal insulation standards, all these measures will erode purchasing power".[1]

He concludes that: "The concept of a happy transition is a utopia. It will entail sacrifices - which, if done right, will be quite reasonable - that will reduce our purchasing power over the next thirty years. Instead of continuing to exploit inexpensive fossil resources, we will have to use energy that is more complex to manage and more expensive to produce. And this will continue for much longer, despite some impressive technological successes".[2]

And he warns: "This will be made all the more difficult by the fact that our attempts to wean ourselves off fossil fuels will be accompanied by a fall in their price on world markets, because the countries that produce this energy will do everything to exploit their fossil fuel reserves, even if it means accepting a fall in their oil, gas or coal revenues".[3]

[1]Gollier, Christian (2019), *Le climat après la fin du mois*, PUF, p. 14–15.

[2]Ibid.

[3]Ibid.

Finally, he asks: "Are the French prepared today to sacrifice a little of their own well-being to greatly improve the well-being of others - even if those others are not French and probably haven't even been born yet?"[4]

Sister Emmanuelle issued this warning: "Driven by a great thirst for ideals, some people can no longer stand the determinants of their lives and seek to escape them. They want to leave everything behind, their families and their studies, to become involved in humanitarian action, in the ecological struggle [...]. They are ready to commit themselves [...] but they want to change the world, and that's impossible. [...] Left to their own devices, any hope of success would be a denial of the human condition, the realisation soon bringing on bitterness and discouragement. They tower dangerously above humanity, and they usually come to a very harsh judgement of everyone [...]. A slippery slope, a source of fanaticism! As Pascal put it: 'Man is neither angel nor beast, unhappily whoever wants to act the angel, acts the beast'".

Carbon Pricing

Like his peers Nicholas Stern (London School of Economics) and Joseph Stiglitz (Columbia University), Christian Gollier considers that there needs to be a universal carbon price of €50 per tonne. His view is that: "This figure takes into account the many facets of this externality, from the loss of biodiversity to the drop in labour and agricultural productivity, as well as the additional cost of air-conditioning buildings in summer, the consequences of rising sea levels, the increase in mortality due to heat waves and hurricanes, and the reduction in life expectancy in the most vulnerable regions".[5]

He adds: "These effects will be extremely spread out over time. One of the difficulties in valuing them arises from this temporal dimension of climate damage, which will affect future generations over several centuries. This means that this measure of €50 per tonne of CO_2 must inevitably depend on judgements about our responsibilities towards future generations".[6]

Christian Gollier invites the reader to visualise a tonne of carbon in the following terms: "One tonne of CO_2 is equivalent to a Paris-New York return flight, a year's gas heating for a three-room flat in Paris, or a 7,000-kilometre journey in a small saloon car".[7]

[4]Ibid.

[5]Ibid.

[6]Ibid.

[7]Ibid.

Endurance

In *Honte*, Hugo Claus [1929–2008] warned: "Only the impatient sets off without having the means to complete his journey. It matters how long it will take, for every moment is indispensable".

Sister Emmanuelle explained: "I think it's good that everyone should feel their helplessness at one time or another". She added: "There comes a day when the projection of one's own success falls apart. Every human should experience this stripping away, however painful it may be. Shorn of his chimeras, shivering, all verbiage and plumage torn off, the bare heart becomes an abyss. Then there is room for truth".

For her: "Life is almost like a fury, a passion for moving forward, walking, climbing, fighting, losing and winning. Winning above all. Life is always about moving forward, banded together, running hand in hand with others." And she added: "Life is a risk; if you haven't risked, you haven't lived. That's what produces ... the sweet taste of champagne".

Sister Emmanuelle admitted: "Life is scarier than death, in fact. It's a bigger unknown". Her advice: "You must not let your life come to a standstill. You have to keep running, and never cease striving. And you always, always prevail".

Reaction

Knowing how to react is essential in business to make optimal decisions and preserve energy, for entrepreneurship is a marathon.

Austria's Hans Selye [1907–1982], who was the first to incorporate the term stress into the medical lexicon to describe the "nonspecific response of the body to any demand",[8] wrote: "It's not stress that kills us, it is our reaction to it." As for Sister Emmanuelle, she had this to say: "I don't know what it is to feel uncomfortable with oneself. I won't abide stress. I simply refuse it. Stress is not living. To live is to walk, to sing!"

Maurice Maeterlinck [1862–1949], who was awarded the 1911 Nobel Prize in Literature, wrote on the same subject as Hans Selye: "There are no miserable events, only events that are miserably received".

[8]Tan, Siang Yong, and Yip, A. (2018), *Hans Selye (1907–1982): Founder of the stress theory, Singapore Medical Journal.*

Economic Freedom

The economist Gustave de Molinari [1819–1912], a disciple of Frédéric Bastiat, considered that economic freedom benefited the consumer: "That in all cases, for all commodities that serve to provide for the tangible or intangible needs of the consumer, it is in the consumer's best interest that labor and trade remain free, because the freedom of labor and of trade have as their necessary and permanent result the maximum reduction of price".[9]

As with all freedoms, economic freedom ends where another's economic freedom begins, as explained in 1884 in *L'évolution politique et la Révolution* by Gustave de Molinari: "Sovereignty rests in the property of the individual over his person and goods and in the liberty of disposing of them. . . . If an individual or a group employ their sovereignty to establish an organization designed to satisfy any need, they have the right. ... This is the sovereign right of the producer. However, this right is naturally limited by the rights of equally sovereign individuals in their dual character as producers and consumers".[10]

Ownership

In 1849, in *Soirées de la Rue Saint Lazare*, Gustave de Molinari has one of the characters, the economist, declare: "Society did not, however, create property, it being rather the case that property created society".[11]

Economic Science

In 1849, Molinari stated: "According to others, on the contrary, society is a purely natural fact. Like the earth on which it stands, society moves in accordance with general, pre-existing laws. In this system, there is no such thing, strictly speaking, as

[9]Molinari, Gustave de (2009), *The Production of Security*, translated by J. Huston McCulloch, Ludwig von Mises Institute. This essay was originally published as *De la production de la sécurité*, in Journal des Economistes (February 1849): 277–90.

[10]https://mises.org/profile/gustave-de-molinari-1

[11]Molinari, Gustave de (1849), L*es Soirées de la Rue Saint-Lazare: Entretiens sur les lois économiques et défense de la propriété*, Paris: Guillaumin. Translation from Readings from the OLL Reader / Gustave de Molinari, "On Socialism and Property Rights" (1849), https://oll.libertyfund.org/page/reader-molinari-socialism

social science; there is only economic science, which studies the natural organism of society and shows how this organism functions".[12]

Christian Gollier [1961–] considers that: "Economics is a combat sport, particularly in France where it is often adjudged to be partisan and non-scientific".

Monetary Policy

Gustave de Molinari's comments about monetary policy remain topical: "Formerly, when governments found themselves unable to pay their debts, they debased their coinage, adding copper or lead to it, or perhaps even reducing the weight of the coins. These days they go about it differently: they borrow large sums from those establishments exclusively authorized, by themselves, to issue paper money. Deprived of its natural and requisite foundation, this money depreciates in times of crisis. The government then intervenes in order to make the public bear the weight of the depreciation".[13]

Taxation

Gustave de Molinari asked: "What does a tax do? It takes either from the producer or the consumer a more or less sizable portion of the product destined in part to consumption and in part to savings, in order to apply it to less productive or even destructive ends, and more rarely to savings. [. . .] It is impossible to know if the price fixed by the government invested with a monopoly in furnishing its services does not unjustly exceed what would have been established through competition. [. . .] But the State possesses an obligatory clientele, so that, whether it raises the prices or lowers the quality of its services, its client cannot refuse them. As ruinous as taxes may be, the State is amply provided with the powers necessary to force him to pay them".[14]

---

[12] Molinari, Gustave de (2009), *The Production of Security*, translated by J. Huston McCulloch, Ludwig von Mises Institute. This essay was originally published as *De la production de la sécurité*, in Journal des Economistes (February 1849): 277–90.

[13] Molinari, Gustave de (1849), *Les Soirées de la Rue Saint-Lazare: Entretiens sur les lois économiques et défense de la propriété*, Paris: Guillaumin. https://oll.libertyfund.org/page/gdm-soirees

[14] Molinari, Gustave de (1911), *Ultima Verba: Mon dernier ouvrage*, Paris: Giard et Brière.

Statism

In *Questions économiques à l'ordre du jour* published in 1906, Gustave de Molinari described what would unfold after the Second World War, warning of the growing weight of the State: "For the time will come when the State, whether it remains in the hands of the conservatives or falls into those of the socialists, will weigh so heavily on society that it will cease to be able to bear it".

Principle of Authority

As explained by Gustave de Molinari: "The moral foundation of authority is neither as solid nor as wide, under a regime of monopoly or of communism, as it could be under a regime of liberty".[15]

Consumer

Consumer protection is nothing new under the sun. Already in 1949, Gustave de Molinari argued that: "The interests of the consumer with regard to any commodity ought to take precedence over the interests of the producer".[16]

Sister Emmanuelle campaigned for small local businesses: "How can small businesses compete with companies the size of Coca-Cola? The power of advertising is attracting a public already fascinated by all things American and foreign, creating new needs and killing off modest national productions. For the same reasons, in wealthy countries, small shops are closing, unable to compete with supermarkets and hypermarkets. The fact is multinationals are accentuating poverty and the dependence of local economies".

[15] Molinari, Gustave de (2009), *The Production of Security*, translated by J. Huston McCulloch, Ludwig von Mises Institute. This essay was originally published as *De la production de la sécurité*, in Journal des Economistes (February 1849): 277–90.

[16] https://mises.org/profile/gustave-de-molinari-1

Monopoly

Gustave de Molinari observed that: "All monopolies are maintained necessarily by force". He warned about the dangers of state monopolies: "A monopoly government is certainly worth no more than that of a grocery shop. The production of security inevitably becomes expensive and of poor quality when it is organized as a monopoly. The monopoly of security is the main cause of the wars which up until our own day have caused such distress to the human race".[17]

[17] Molinari, Gustave de (1849), *Les Soirées de la Rue Saint-Lazare: Entretiens sur les lois économiques et défense de la propriété*, Paris: Guillaumin. Translation from Readings from the OLL Reader / Gustave de Molinari, *On Socialism and Property Rights* (1849), https://oll.libertyfund.org/page/reader-molinari-socialism

Bulgaria

Crises and Cycles

In *Les crises périodiques de surproduction*,[1] Albert Aftalion [1874–1956] explained fluctuations or oscillations in the market economy as follows: "Prosperity leads to the crisis. Depression brings prosperity back".

> Because of the conditions created by capitalist technique, prices dictate production and production dictates prices in such a way that industry is caught up in an endless chain of actions and reactions which constitute economic cycles.

Accelerator Effect or Stove Metaphor

Albert Aftalion explained economic fluctuations by what is called the real sphere of the economy, namely business investment. To represent this mechanism, Aftalion used the stove metaphor.

If a room has a stove and a window and occupants complain about the cold, the immediate reaction is to stoke up the stove. Since coal is slow to ignite, there is a tendency to overfill. As a result, when the fire gets going, the room will become unbearably hot. The reaction is to open the window to let in outside air, bringing the room back to its original temperature. And so on... Similarly, in the economy, businesses, seeing reserves of purchasing power, invest. In doing so, they increase not only production capacity but also demand, which deceives them about the reality of the opportunities existing in the economy and encourages them to amplify the investment dynamic, in his metaphor to stoke up the stove. Overinvestment and the pursuit of a strategy to meet a need that has already been filled combine to cause a

[1] *Periodic Crises of Overproduction.*

C. Peicuti, *The European Economy in 100 Quotes*, Contributions to Economics,
https://doi.org/10.1007/978-3-031-68819-5_22

crisis. Reducing investment brings capital back to a level that matches needs, which reduces the amplitude of the crisis. The amplifying effect of investment on growth is called the “accelerator effect”.

Gender Financial Equality

In *Les lois relatives à l'épargne de la femme mariée: leur importance pour la protection de l'épouse dans les classes laborieuses*[2] published in 1898, Albert Aftalion, who completed a doctorate in law at the University of Paris, was concerned about the status of married women, which he described as: “One of the most painful problems, and one that requires the quickest resolution”.

He drew attention to the precarious economic situation of “working-class wives” and their children as a result of the abuse of the law: “Publicists and jurisconsults agree in deploring the situation of a woman who is subjected, without effective protection, to the extensive powers of a husband who is sometimes unworthy. Her wages and savings, which are essential for her upkeep and that of her children, are legally at the disposal of the husband, who is the sole judge as to their use, being free to dissipate them in a dissolute life if seen fit. Various attempts have been made to find a remedy against possible abuses by husbands”.

Women's Savings

The Caisses d'Épargne, whose origins go back to the founding in 1818 of the Caisse d'Épargne et de Prévoyance de Paris, allowed women to open a savings book without the consent of their husbands back in 1881. In the preface to *Les lois relatives à l'épargne de la femme mariée: leur importance pour la protection de l'épouse dans les classes laborieuses*, Aftalion paid tribute to the Caisses d'Épargne for going further in the application of the law than was required: “But in all these efforts to improve the lot of the married woman, attempts already made in the same direction are unjustly neglected; in particular, the recent laws concerning the Caisses d'Épargne are forgotten, or only spoken of disdainfully. The help they have brought to poor women is dismissed as paltry or illusory. The suggestion is that the right conferred on women to have savings of their own is a mere tolerance, which the husband is free to put an end to. It is true that in some respects this opinion is justified by the text of law concerning the Caisses d'Épargne”.

---

[2]https://gallica.bnf.fr/ark:/12148/bpt6k5461901f/f9.item.r=Cours%20d'economie%20politique%20Albert%20Aftalion%20 (1874–1956).

Aftalion went on to observe: "But laws often undergo a profound transformation when they move from written form to concrete implementation. When they come into contact with facts, theoretical principles lose their abstract clarity. They are sometimes adapted to reality only by losing their original rigour and generality. As a result of circumstances, under the influence of certain necessities, or through their combination with other legal principles, they take on a character quite different from that intended, and they achieve a purpose for which they were not created. All codification is powerless to stop the secret and continuous development in the legislation of an unwritten law, of a customary law".

Aftalion then paid tribute to the Caisses d'Épargne, which went further than the law to establish financial equality between women and men: "These ideas are borne out by those articles of laws concerning the Caisses d'Épargne relating to married women. Immediately after these laws were promulgated, de facto practices, or 'customs' as they might be called, were established that extended women's rights in ways not anticipated. The freedom to save, completely independent of any marital intervention, which the law had refused the married woman, was not far from having been granted to her in its entirety by practice. The poor married woman was called upon to participate alongside the husband, within fairly broad limits relative to the modest resources of the household, in the governance of the family's financial interests. In this matter, we can see in the contrast between the laws and practice an experiment in legislation that is not devoid of lessons".

Aftalion concluded on the application of the law by the Caisses d'Épargne with these words: "In reality, practice more or less openly restricts the husband's rights in favour of the wife. The husband's prerogatives remain intact as long as he has not authorised his wife's first payment. However, once he has done so, he loses his superior power. The wife may continue to make deposits despite the husband's wishes to the contrary. She can also prevent any repayment of deposits that she considers inappropriate. [...] In this way, serious protection was guaranteed to working-class women".

Joint Bank Accounts

Aftalion also mentioned another key measure taken by the Caisses d'Épargne to promote gender equality, at a time when the law recognised the husband as wielding marital power: "However, an even more far-reaching exception was made to the Civil Code. The Caisses d'Épargne must refuse any repayment to one of the spouses, to the husband or wife acting alone. The bank can only return the sums deposited to both spouses. If only one of them goes to the branch, he or she must obtain the written consent of the spouse. The husband may wield marital power, yet he is unable to collect amounts payable to the couple; contrary to the principles, he can only do so in conjunction with his spouse".

Account Opening

Aftalion explained that Caisses d'Épargne opened accounts for married women under their maiden name to enable them to freely dispose of their money: "It is true that, by a somewhat roundabout means, the married woman was able to deposit and withdraw money without her husband's involvement. By arranging for an account to be opened in her maiden name, the married woman had no restrictions on her freedom. The local branch manager, unaware or pretending to be unaware of her married status, did not worry about the husband's marital power over the funds entrusted to the bank's safekeeping".

Aftalion added: "It seems that the Caisses d'Épargne were quite willing to accept the veracity of such statements from a married woman. An almost general practice developed along these lines. This practice would often be recalled in the debates that took place in Parliament on the subject of the law concerning the Caisses d'Épargne".

Aftalion went on to cite examples: "It has been said that the right to deposit without prior authorisation exists, but that it exists in an irregular manner".[3] Also: "When amounts are deposited by women at the Caisses d'Épargne, their deposits are not refused, and when amounts are withdrawn by them, their withdrawals are not refused either... The passbook gives the wife's name, but it does not specifically indicate the husband's name".[4]

Concerning the last example, Aftalion pointed out: "This last sentence may be seen as an admission of the procedure used by the banks to derogate from the fundamental principles of the Civil Code in favour of the married woman. However, it must be recognised that in this way, whatever the circumstances of the case, which often excused the habits of the Caisses d'Épargne, they were acting totally outside the law. It would therefore seem desirable that legislation be passed to enshrine and, above all, to complete the protection afforded to married women by practice".

It would take 84 years for the wish of the eminent economist and jurist to be fulfilled in France, the Law of 13 July 1965 finally completing the French women's journey toward financial independence.

---

[3]Footnote to the original French text: *Discours de M. Tallon à l'Assemblée nationale, séance du 15 mai 1875 (Journal officiel du 16).*

[4]Footnote to the original French text: *Discours de M. Robert de Massy au Sénat, séance du 28 mars 1881 (Journal officiel du 29).*

Money

Banker, industrialist, and statesman Atanas Burov [1875–1954] stated: "It is clear for any person of sound mind that before wealth can be shared, it must be created".

For him: "The great task of a government is to create the means for accumulating more goods, more wealth, so that the common wealth, and therefore private wealth, can be increased".

He considered that: "Strengthened production requires as a precondition an elevated working class, a working class that is materially secure, culturally educated, that feels it is in its interest to maintain and increase production".

He delivered this analysis: "Money corrupts the small man and elevates the great man. It does not corrupt man".

The writer, humorist, artist, and historian Chudomir, born Dimitar Hristov Chorbadzhiyski [1890–1967], said: "If you want to know the price of money, try borrowing some".

The writer, scriptwriter and journalist Pavel Vezhinov [1914–1983] considered that: "As long as there is money in this world, people will remain insignificant and mean-spirited".

For him: "Money has no face and no appearance; it becomes like the person who handles it. There's dirty money, worthless money, pitiful money. And then there's money that's worthless, that you can't buy anything with. That's miserly money".

Editor, lawyer, and professor Yaroslav Radev [1920–2009], who served as vice-president of the State Council, considered that: "Money is a personal document attesting to the inequality of people".

His view was that: "The greedy always lack something. Excess breeds greed. Greed increases wealth, but destroys the man".

And also that: "Wealth circumvents the law".

According to the journalist Vasil Karakashev [1934–2018]: "Money is like politicians. Every spin of the wheel brings its recompense".

The playwright, poet, and satirist Veselin Georgiev [1935–] stated: "Your money runs out quickly, other people's money never does!"

According to the writer and humorist Zhivko Sotirov [1936–]: "The rich make money. The poor make children".

The writer, ethnographer, and politician Stiliyan Chilingirov [1881–1962] wrote: "When you give someone a little, they become your debtor; when you give them a lot, you are in their debt".

According to Beron: "We asked a merchant: how do you do to earn so much money? To which he replied: much is easy, a little difficult".

Corruption

The writer, poet, and satirist Radoy Ralin [1923–2004] contended that: "If the people won't be bought lock, stock, and barrel, they will be corrupted".

For the poet Ivan Arnaudov [1932–]: "A corrupted policeman is more dangerous than a bandit".

For Karakashev: "The dirtiest things are done with laundered money".

According to the writer, poet, and politician Petar Anastasov [1942–2023]: "Corruption in high places remains out of reach of the law as if an omnipotent, omnibenevolent boss were watching over it".

War

According to Ralin: "Statesmen, when they have totally pillaged their subjects, will convince them to invade foreign countries".

Poverty

According to Ralin: "Poverty is not a vice, but a lesson".

Stoyan Stoyanov [1929–2009] considered that: "Where everybody is poor, nobody begs".

His view is that: "The poor must rapidly forget his humiliation, for every day he must beg for bread".

For the writer Alexi Andreev [1930–1995]: “No recompense is ever as generous as it seems”.

The Bulgarian translator and writer Zdravka Evtimova [1959–] said: “I am ashamed to be powerless in the face of poverty”.

The encyclopaedist, educationalist, philosopher, and naturalist Petar Beron [1779–1871] believed that: “If you don’t save, you soon become poor”.

Anastasov declared: “The poverty of a great part of the Bulgarian population is humiliating not just for Bulgarians, but also for humanity in general”.

Malta

Establishment

The Order of St. John dates back to 1048. It is said that merchants from the ancient Marine Republic of Amalfi obtained from the Caliph of Egypt the authorisation to build in Jerusalem, a church, a convent, and a hospital to care for pilgrims of any religious faith or race. The Order of St. John of Jerusalem became an independent monastic community that ran the hospital for the pilgrims travelling to the Holy Land. It became a lay religious order in 1113. It later moved to the island of Malta, granted to the Order by Charles V, then established its Conventual Seat in Rhodes, becoming successively the Order of Rhodes, then of Malta.

According to Frà Cesare Magalotti, the Order was "a sacred, ecclesiastical Republic, the flower of the most select and the most eminent nobility of all Christendom".[1]

Giovanni Francesco Abela [1582–1655], a Maltese noble who rose to the rank of Vice Chancellor of the Order of the Knights of the Hospital of Saint John of Jerusalem, commonly known as the Knights Hospitaller, was the author of the first book on the history and geography of Malta.[2] In the book's dedication, the author stressed that Malta should be proud "to have become the royal palace of the Holy Religion of Jerusalem, that is to say of the best-chosen blood of all Christendom". The ancestry of the nobility had been the subject of an institutional examination by the Order since its creation.

[1] https://www.orderofmalta.int/wp-content/uploads/2022/02/2017-Hospitaller-Web-Edition.pdf

[2] Abela, Giovanni Francesco (1647). *Della Descrittione di Malta isola nel Mare Siciliano: con le sue antichità, ed altre notizie*, Malta: Paolo Bonacota.

C. Peicuti, *The European Economy in 100 Quotes*, Contributions to Economics,
https://doi.org/10.1007/978-3-031-68819-5_23

Napoléon Bonaparte, the then Commander in Chief of the Army of the Orient, captured Malta in June 1798. Had the 300 knights, in majority French, even had the means to withstand a long siege, they had no wish to fight Bonaparte, and they surrendered on 12 June 1798. That proved a strategic error, for the Order represented the Ancient Regime in the eyes of Bonaparte.

On 13 June, France provided Malta with a constitution, created municipalities, and granted French citizenship to all of the island's inhabitants; feudal privileges and slavery were abolished. The church's extensive property and works of art were confiscated, and the French troops would later loot church property. On 14 June, Napoleon ordered the expulsion of the Knights Hospitaller, who would disperse after that. On 17 June, Bonaparte informed the Directoire that: "We have in the centre of the Mediterranean the strongest fortress in Europe, and it will cost anyone dear to dislodge us".

On 18 June, Bonaparte set sail for Egypt, leaving behind a garrison of 4000 men on the island of Malta.

International Hospitaller Mission

In 1834, the Order settled definitively in Rome, where it enjoyed extraterritorial status.

The Order of Malta conducts its operations through 11 priories, 48 national associations, 133 diplomatic missions, 1 worldwide relief agency, and 33 national volunteer corps, as well as numerous hospitals, medical centres, and specialist foundations. It does not pursue any economic or political goal and does not depend on any other state or government. Its mission is: "Upholding human dignity and caring for people in need".[3]

"Its 13,500 members, 95,000 permanent volunteers and qualified staff of 52,000 professionals—most of whom are medical personnel and paramedics—form an efficient network that includes everything from emergency relief for refugees and the displaced living through war and conflict, to intervention in areas hit by natural disasters, hospital work, medical care and social services.

Its programmes, run independently or within a framework of partnerships with governments and international agencies, are now active in 120 countries.

[3] https://www.orderofmaltafederal.org/mission

Aid for the victims of natural catastrophes and armed conflicts has intensified in recent decades".[4]

The Order of Malta has its own diplomatic network: "The diplomatic relations which the Sovereign Order of Malta enjoys with 112 countries and the European Union, its permanent observer status at the United Nations and international Cooperation Agreements concluded with over 50 states, exist to facilitate its humanitarian activities, and allow unrestricted and protected access, especially in crisis regions.

The Order's diplomatic network strengthens its relationships with the governments of the countries in which it operates. This network allows its medical programmes to be integrated into national and regional healthcare systems and to facilitate the importing of healthcare equipment to reach people in need as quickly as possible".[5]

Its longstanding independence and standing in the international community means that the Order can play the role of mediator: "Due to its status as a neutral, apolitical and independent institution and its humanitarian role and ongoing activities in 120 countries, the Sovereign Order of Malta is able to intervene as a mediator in conflicts".[6]

---

[4] https://www.orderofmalta.int/humanitarian-medical-works/hospitaller-mission/

[5] https://www.orderofmalta.int/diplomatic-activities/

[6] Ibid.

Spain

Wealth

The novelist, playwright, poet, and soldier Miguel de Cervantes [1547–1616] considered that: "The gratification of wealth is not found in mere possession or lavish expenditure, but in its wise application".

The poet, lyricist, and satirist Luis de Góngora y Argote [1561–1627], about the financial mismanagement of the heirs of great fortunes, wrote: "That a rich greedy one gathers the doubloons a hundred to one hundred may well be; more than the gentile successor does not spend thousands to a thousand, it cannot be".

King Philip II of Spain [1527–1598] stated: "Receive what is yours and pass on to the next man what is his".

For the Spanish journalist and author Josep Pla i Casadevall [1897–1981]: "Money doesn't bring happiness, of course, but neither is it a serious obstacle".

According to playwright Jacinto Benavente [1866–1954]: "Money cannot make us happy, but it is the only thing that compensates us for not being happy".

He also wrote: "The fact that money doesn't make you happy is what the rich say so that the poor don't envy them too much".

Pablo Picasso [1881–1973] stated: "I'd like to live as a poor man with lots of money". He was speaking from experience; as explained by historian Annie Cohen-Solal in her book *Picasso the Foreigner: An Artist in France, 1900–1973*, Picasso was extremely poor for much of his life.

C. Peicuti, *The European Economy in 100 Quotes*, Contributions to Economics,
https://doi.org/10.1007/978-3-031-68819-5_24

The Spanish writer and professor of literature Gonzalo Torrente Ballester [1910–1999] explained that: "When money is at stake, freedom is very difficult to attain".

Writer, playwright, and priest Calderón de la Barca [1600–1681] stated: "Don't ever proffer advice to someone who's asking you for money".

Writer and politician Francisco Gomez de Quevedo [1580–1645] wrote: "Lord Money is a powerful knight".

There are many Catalan sayings about the subject of money:

A gambler's bag has no straps.

Don't go to the fair if you're penniless, for you'll see many things but return empty-handed.

You won't have to ask anyone for the money you've saved.

The father earns, the son spends.

Never be the first to speak, to pour water, or to give money.

He who has health and money lacks nothing.

Ferrymen and innkeepers make money.

Money won gambling will get you nowhere.

With money in your hand, you'll make the whole world dance.

Money and meals will prize open even doors stuck shut.

With money in your hand, demons become saints.

With women and money, show the utmost caution.

Love without money is a brief affair.

Arms and money require sound handling.

Money and firewood are not handed out free anywhere.

Money and good manners won't be yours overnight.

What can't be achieved with money won't be achieved with anything else.

Money that you don't earn working has to be earned crying.

Money is like fruits, harder to keep than to pluck.

Lessons on how to earn money are taught by those who have none.

In contrast to the French who believe that "*les bons comptes font les bons amis*", or as the English would say "short reckonings make long friends", Catalans consider that "when it's friends, you don't count".

Eat a grape at each chime of the clock at midnight on New Year's eve will bring money all year.

To be rich is not to have heaps of money but to live a contented life.

When you run out of money, you must rely on yourself and no one else.

When the wife has money, the husband has even more.

With my money, I would be Pope.

For a woman to desire you, give her all the money and let her do what she wants.

If you want to know someone's inner self, give them power and money.

Fortune

According to Francisco de Quevedo [1580–1645]: "He is not happy to whom fortune can no longer give anything, but he to whom it can take nothing away".

Several Catalan saying on the subject of fortune:

He dances well when fortune plucks the guitar's cords.

Don't oppose fortune and love.

Too much time gazing at the moon won't leave enough to make your fortune.

Time, wind, women and fortune all rotate like the moon.

You still want to be rich? Spend one-hundredth of what you earn.

Poor

Francisco de Quevedo wrote: "The rich eat, the poor nourish themselves".

Poverty features large in Catalan sayings:

To the poor knowledge, to the rich ignorance.

A well-managed household keeps poverty away.

Money at Christmas, poverty come the summer solstice.

There are three types of misfortunes: disease, poverty and hail.

Pride and poverty don't fit in the same bag.

Laziness is the mother of poverty.

Poverty has no friends; wealth has enemies.

There's no better teacher than necessity.

Living free in poverty is worth more than imprisonment with wealth.

Truth

In Catalonia, there is a saying that: "In business, not always telling the truth does you a disservice".

Francisco Suarez [1545–1617], one of the leading figures of the School of Salamanca movement, warned: "The greater the truth, the greater the libel".

Value

According to Miguel de Cervantes: "Abundance, even of good things prevents them from being valued; and scarcity, even in the case of what is bad, confers a certain value".

In *De jure et justitia*, Luis de Molina [1535–1600], a member of the School of Salamanca, explained that: "Value is not a property of goods, but a reflection of how people use them".

In *Veterum Collatio Numismatum,* cum *his, quae modo expenduntur, publica, et Regia authoritate perpensa*, Diego de Covarrubia [1512–1577], another member of the School of Salamanca, had this to say: "The value of an article does not depend on its essential nature but on the subjective estimation of men, even if that estimation is wild".[1]

Price

In *Instruccion de mercaderes*, Luis Saravia de la Calle [1500–1550], a member of the School of Salamanca, defined the just price as follows: "Excluding all deceit and malice, the just price of a thing is the price which it commonly fetches at the time and place of the deal, in cash".[2]

Tomás de Mercado [1525–1575], a member of the School of Salamanca, stated: "The just price is the one that is publicly agreed, used this week and this hour, as said

[1]Covarrubias, Diego de (1604), *Veterum Collatio Numismatum,* cum *his, quae modo expenduntur, publica, et Regia authoritate perpensa*, Omnia Opera pp. 669–710.

[2]Calle, Luis Saravia de la (1544), *Instruccion de mercaderes*, Medina del Campo, from Grice-Hutchinson. Marjorie (1952), *The School of Salamaca, Readings in Spanish Monetary Theory 1544–1605*, Oxford at the Clarendon Press.

in the marketplace, without force or deceit, though experience shows it will be more changing than wind".

Ownership

Francisco de Vitoria [1480–1546], a member of the School of Salamanca, considered that there was a right of ownership, but that: "Nobody owns things in such a way that he will never have to share them at some point. That is to say, man should not own external things as if they were his but rather as if they were common, in such a way that one can easily share them to meet other's needs".[3]

In *Relectio C. novit de iudiciis non minus sublimis quam celebris pronunciata an MDXLVIII*, Martin de Azpilcueta [1491–1586], a member of the School of Salamanca, wrote: "The kingdom does not belong to the king, but to the community; by virtue of natural law, royal power belongs to the community and not to the king; therefore the community can never wholly abdicate that power".[4]

Luis de Molina warned that: "When a donkey is owned by many, it will soon be meat to the wolves".

Inflation

In *Manual de confesores y penitentes*, Martin de Azpilcueta explained that: "Money is worth more where and when it is scarce than where and when it is abundant". He added that: "The abundance of money leads to higher prices, which has a very negative impact on society".

Honour

Francisco de Vitoria considered that: "Honour is the deference owed to virtue".

Francisco Gomez de Quevedo believed that: "He who loses honour for business, loses business and honour".

---

[3] Alcolea, Lucas Clover (2023), *The Problem of Property: Looking Back to the 'Dark Ages' to Get Through the Dark Ages*, University of St. Thomas Journal of Law and Public Policy, Volume 16.

[4] Azpilcueta, Martín de (1576), *Relectio C. novit de iudiciis non minus sublimis quam celebris pronunciata an MDXLVIII*, Apud Gulielmun Rovillium, from Chap. 6, Martin de Azpilcueta, by Wim Decock, Great Christian Jurists in Spanish History (Law and Christianity) (2018), edited by Rafael Domingo and Javier Martínez-Torrón.

Strategy

Francisco de Vitoria has these words of advice: "If a shield suffices to your defence, don't raise your sword".

He insisted that: "One may not commit bad deeds, even to avoid worst ills".

War

Francisco de Vitoria stated: "Difference of religion is not a cause of just war".[5]

Collectivism

Francisco de Vitoria drew attention to the fact that: "If the goods are put in common, it will be the wicked, even the greedy and thieves, who would benefit most. They would take more and put less in the community granary".

Sale Contract

Francisco de Vitoria explained that: "In its essence, the sale seems established in the common interest of the buyer and seller by mutual need, since each has something the other needs. Therefore, the contract should be based on the equality of the thing (*secundum aequalitatem rei*), as what was established in the common interest should not be to the detriment of one of the parties".

Governance

The Jesuit philosopher and theologian Francisco Suarez [1545–1617] wrote: "If, then, a lawful king is ruling in tyrannical fashion, and if the state finds at hand no other means of self-defence than the expulsion and deposition of this king, the said

[5] Vitoria, Francisco de (1532), *De Indis*, https://theahi.org/wp-content/uploads/2013/10/Francisco-de-Vitoria-on-War.pdf

state, acting as a whole, and in accordance with the public and general deliberations of the communities and leading men, may depose him".[6]

He also added that: "Human law takes its legitimacy from its conformity with natural law".

Ecology

According to Francisco Suarez: "The first law of nature is self-preservation, and the second is the preservation of the species".

Perseverance

For Miguel de Cervantes: "The closer the desired good is to the hope of possessing it, the greater the fatigue".

Progress

Spanish writer Miguel Delibes [1920–2010] considered that: "Progress does not work ... if it has to translate inexorably into an increase of isolation and violence, of autocracy and mistrust, of injustice and prostitution of the natural environment, of the exploitation of man by man and the exaltation of money as the only value".

Savings

According to Miguel Delibes: "Savings, when achieved at the cost of an unmet need, cause the acrimony and bitterness of the people".

One Catalan saying is about savings: "With work and savings, the farm will grow".

Need

For our greed, much is too little; for our need, much is way more than enough.

[6] Suarez, Francisco (1613), *A Defence of the Catholic and Apostolic Faith in Refutation of the Errors of the Anglican Sect, with a Reply to the Apologie for the Oath of Allegiance and to the admonitory Preface of His Most Serene Majesty James, King of England.*

Poland

If, in 1946, the future Nobel laureate Milton Friedman wrote a lengthy critique of the work of Oskar Lange [1904–1965] that was published in the leading US economic review, it is because the work of the Polish economist was known the world over. While Milton Friedman conceded that Oskar Lange was an "able and careful [. . .] theorist", he questioned his methodology: "The basic sources of the defects in Lange's theoretical analysis are the emphasis on formal structure, the attempt to generalize without first specifying in detail the facts to be generalized, and the failure to recognize that the ultimate test of the validity of a theory is not conformity to the canons of formal logic but the ability to deduce facts that have not yet been observed, that are capable of being contradicted by observation, and that subsequent observation does not contradict".[1]

Needs

According to Oskar Lange: "Human needs, although originally derived from biological necessity, are thus a result of the existence of society and are conditioned by the stage of development which society has reached".[2]

[1]Friedman, Milton (1946), *Lange on Price Flexibility and Employment: A Methodological Criticism*, The American Economic Review, Vol. 36, No. 4, September 1946.

[2]Lange, Oskar (2013), *Political Economy, Volume I: General Problems*, Elsevier.

C. Peicuti, *The European Economy in 100 Quotes*, Contributions to Economics,
https://doi.org/10.1007/978-3-031-68819-5_25

Economic Science

Oskar Lange stressed that economic science is objective: "Our conclusion about the objectivity of economic science may seem startling. Economists are rather notorious for being unable to reach agreement and for being divided into opposing 'schools of thought,' 'orthodox' and 'unorthodox,' 'bourgeois' and 'socialist,' and many others. The existence of profound disagreement among economists, however, does not refute our thesis about the objectivity of economics as a science".[3]

Carl Menger [1840–1921] defined the economy as follows: "Man himself is the beginning and the end of every economy".[4]

Socialism

Oskar Lange believed in market socialism but acknowledged that: "It seems to us, indeed, that the real danger of socialism is that of a bureaucratization of economic life".[5]

Value

Carl Menger is known for his "subjective theory of value": "When I discussed the nature of value, I observed that value is nothing inherent in goods and that it is not a property of goods. But neither is value an independent thing. There is no reason why a good may not have value to one economizing individual but no value to another individual under different circumstances. The measure of value is entirely subjective in nature, and for this reason a good can have great value to one economizing individual, little value to another, and no value at all to a third, depending upon the differences in their requirements and available amounts. What one person disdains or values lightly is appreciated by another, and what one person abandons is often picked up by another.[6]

[3]Lange, Oskar (1945–1946), *The Scope and Method of Economics*, The Review of Economic Studies, Vol. 13, No. 1 (1945–1946).

[4]Menger, Carl (1871), *On the Origins of Money*, Ludwig von Mises Institute, in the preface by Douglas E. French.

[5]Lange, Oskar (1937), *On the Economic Theory of Socialism*, Review of Economic Studies, Vol. IV, Nos. 1 and 2 (October, 1936, and February, 1937).

[6]Menger, Carl (1871), *Principles of Economics*, Ludwig von Mises Institute.

Menger concluded that: "It is a judgment economizing men make about the importance of the goods at their disposal for the maintenance of their lives and well-being. Hence value does not exist outside the consciousness of men".[7]

Money

According to Carl Menger: "Money is not an invention of the state. It is not the product of a legislative act. Even the sanction of political authority is not necessary for its existence. Certain commodities came to be money quite naturally, as the result of economic relationships that were independent of the power of the state".[8]

Market Price

Menger considered that: "It is an error in economics, as prevalent as it is patent, that all commodities, at a definite point of time and in a given market, may be assumed to stand to each other in a definite relation of exchange, in other words, may be mutually exchanged in definite quantities at will. [. . .] The most cursory observation of market phenomena teaches us that it does not lie within our power, when we have bought an article for a certain price, to sell it again forthwith at the same price".[9]

Michal Kalecki [1899–1970] believed that: "Generally speaking, changes in the prices of finished goods are 'cost determined' while changes in the prices of raw materials inclusive of primary foodstuffs are 'demand determined'".[10]

Economic System

According to Michal Kalecki: "The workers spend what they get, and capitalists get what they spend".[11]

---

[7] Ibid.

[8] Ibid.

[9] Menger, Carl (1871), *On the Origins of Money*, Ludwig von Mises Institute, in the preface by Douglas E. French.

[10] Kalecki, Michal (1954), *Theory of Economic Dynamics: An Essay on Cyclical and Long-Run Changes in Capitalist Economy*, Allen and Unwin, University of Michigan.

[11] Ibid.

According to Oskar Lange: "No scientific law applies when its prerequisite conditions do not occur. Since the administration of scarce resources is influenced by social organisation and institutions, such organisation and institutions are among the conditions implied in economic laws. Consequently, economic laws which hold under one type of social organisation may fail to do so under another type. Most economic laws are thus 'limited historically' to certain given types of social organisation and institutions".[12]

Going on to write: "This, however, does not imply any basic difference between the laws of economics (or of other social sciences) and the laws of the natural sciences. The latter, too, are contingent upon conditions which are subject to change. Different laws of the natural sciences have different degrees of historic permanence, usually a much higher one than the laws of economics, though even this is not always the case (some laws of meteorology are less permanent than some laws of economics). The differences is but one of degree. Like all scientific laws, economic laws are established in order to make successful prediction of the outcome of human actions".[13]

Poor

Kalecki observed that: "An increase in the number of paupers does not broaden the market".[14]

Fiscal Deficit

Michal Kalecki considered that: "In any case of the budget deficit the private sector of the economy receives more from government expenditure than it pays in taxes".[15]

---

[12]Lange, Oskar (1945–1946), *The Scope and Method of Economics*, The Review of Economic Studies, Vol. 13, No. 1 (1945–1946).

[13]Ibid.

[14]Kalecki, Michal (1954), *Theory of Economic Dynamics: An Essay on Cyclical and Long-Run Changes in Capitalist Economy*, Allen and Unwin, University of Michigan.

[15]Ibid.

Monopoly

Michal Kalecki stated: "We have found that the degree of monopoly is likely to increase somewhat during depressions".[16]

Growth

Michal Kalecki wrote: "It may thus be concluded that in the absence of 'development factors' the system lapses into a stationary state. These factors thus appear to be a prerequisite of a steady growth".[17]

State Shareholder

The Polish economist Leszek Henryk Balcerowicz [1947–], who was the President of the Narodowy Bank Polski from 2001 to 2007, considers that: "State ownership tends to be politicised and politicians are not good owners because they tend to avoid to do the necessary measures".[18]

[16] Ibid.

[17] Ibid.

[18] https://www.reuters.com/article/poland-coal-idUSL5N11V39X20151001

Ireland

Work

In *The Remarkable Rocket*, author, playwright, and poet Oscar Wilde [1854–1900] wrote: "I have always been of the opinion that hard work is simply the refuge of people who have nothing whatever to do".

Richard Cantillon [1680–1734] defined the value of work thus: "The labor of an adult slave of the lowest class is worth at least as much as the quantity of land that the owner is obliged to allot for his food and necessities".[1]

An Irish proverb invites us to start work bright and early: *Má chailleann tú uair ar maidin beidh tú á tóraíocht i rith an lae* ("If you lose an hour in the morning, you will be looking for it all day").

In a similar vein: *Tús maith leath na hoibre* ("A good start is half the work").

Vision

In *Thoughts on Various Subjects, Moral and Diverting* published in 1706, Jonathan Swift [1667–1745] wrote: "Vision is the art of seeing things invisible". No less is demanded of the entrepreneur.

William Butler Yeats [1865–1939] considered that: "Talent perceives differences; genius, unity".

[1] Cantillon, Richard (2010), *An Essay on Economic Theory*, Translated by Chantal Saucier, Edited by Mark Thornton, Mises Institute.

C. Peicuti, *The European Economy in 100 Quotes*, Contributions to Economics,
https://doi.org/10.1007/978-3-031-68819-5_26

Counsel

In *Directions to Servants*, published posthumously in 1745, Jonathan Swift observed that: "No man will take counsel, but every man will take money. Therefore, money is better than counsel".

Oscar Wilde urged: "Give neither counsel nor salt till you are asked for it".

Adversity

Great entrepreneurs often have to toil in the face of adversity.

According to Jonathan Swift: "When a true genius appears in the world, you may know him by this sign, that the dunces are all in confederacy against him".

In the play *Annajanska* by George Bernard Shaw [1856–1950], one of the characters exclaims: "All great truths begin as blasphemies".

George Bernard Shaw wrote that: "When you do something, you're up against those who wanted to do it in your place, those who wanted to do the opposite, and those who wanted nothing to be done".

Edna O'Brien [1930–] considers that: "The vote means nothing to women. We should be armed".

Enemies

Oscar Wilde said: "I choose my friends for their good looks, my acquaintances for their good characters, and my enemies for their intellects. A man cannot be too careful in the choice of his enemies".

Value

For Oscar Wilde: "The true perfection of man lies not in what man has, but in what man is".

Money

Oscar Wilde observed that: "There is only one class in the community that thinks more about money than the rich, and that is the poor".

He stated: "When I was young I thought that money was the most important thing in life; now that I am old I know that it is".

George Bernard Shaw considered that: "The surest way to ruin a man who doesn't know how to handle money is to give him some".

Wealth

As pointed out by Oscar Wilde, it is often the rich who are in debt: "The biggest advantage of wealth is that it allows you to get in debt".

Strategy

Oscar Wilde said ironically: "One should always play fairly when one has the winning cards".

In *Ulysses*, Irish novelist, poet, and literary critic James Joyce [1882–1941] wrote: "Errors are volitional and are the portals of discovery".

William Yeats gave the following advice: "Do not wait to strike till the iron is hot; but make it hot by striking".

George Bernard Shaw wrote: "The golden rule is that there are no golden rules".

In *Man and Superman*, he also wrote: "Those who can, do; those who can't, teach". This is particularly true of economics.

George Bernard Shaw considered that: "Mankind would have been happy long ago if men had put all their genius not into repairing their mistakes, but into not committing them". In other words, prevention is better than cure.

According to William Yeats: "Life is a long preparation for something that never happens".

Success

According to George Bernard Shaw, success does not last: “Man can climb to the highest summits, but he cannot dwell there long”.

The Irish playwright defined success as follows: “Success does not consist in never making mistakes but in never making the same one a second time”.

According to Oliver Goldsmith [1728–1774]: “Success consists of getting up just one more time than you fall”.

Fashion

The business model of the luxury industry is based on the perpetual renewal of fashion, which made Oscar Wilde wryly remark in *The Philosophy of Dress*: “Fashion is a form of ugliness so intolerable that we have to alter it every six months”.

For George Bernard Shaw: “A fashion is nothing but an induced epidemic”.

War

War is an exogenous shock that disrupts the economy and often triggers inflation. In *The Critic as Artist*, Oscar Wilde considered that: “As long as war is regarded as wicked, it will always have its fascination. When it is looked upon as vulgar, it will cease to be popular”.

In the preface to *Saint Joan*, George Bernard Shaw wrote about war: “Men are more largely dispensable, and are sacrificed accordingly”.

Endurance

In *Malloy*, Samuel Beckett [1906–1989] wrote: “To major things the surest road is on the minor pains bestowed, if you don’t happen to be in a hurry”.

George Bernard Shaw considered that: “If the English can survive their food, they can survive anything”.

Communication

William Yeats wrote: "Think like a wise man but communicate in the language of the people".

Teamwork

William Yeats gave the following advice: "Choose your companions from the best; who draws a bucket with the rest soon topples down the hill".

George Bernard Shaw explained: "If you have an apple and I have an apple and we exchange apples then you and I will still each have one apple. But if you have an idea and I have an idea and we exchange these ideas, then each of us will have two ideas".

There is an Irish proverb about how two people make light work: *Giorraíonn beirt bóthar* ("Two people shorten the road").

As so aptly summed up by Oscar Wilde: "Some cause happiness wherever they go; others whenever they go".

Education

According to William Yeats: "Education is not the filling of a pail, but the lighting of a fire".

George Bernard Shaw wrote: "When a man teaches something he does not know to somebody else who has no aptitude for it, and gives him a certificate of proficiency, the latter has completed the education of a gentleman".

Compromise

To illustrate what the English believed to be a compromise, William Yeats wrote: "You know what the Englishman's idea of compromise is? He says, Some people say there is a God. Some people say there is no God. The truth probably lies somewhere between these two statements".

Progress

In *Maxims for Revolutionists*, George Bernard Shaw explained that: "The reasonable man adapts himself to the world; the unreasonable one persists in trying to adapt the world to himself. Therefore, all progress depends on the unreasonable man".

In the same brief and thought-provoking book, the author wrote: "Decadence can find agents only when it wears the mask of progress".

Nobel Prize

George Bernard Shaw was awarded the Nobel Prize for Literature in 1925 for *Saint Joan*, but refused the money, observing: "Nobel Prize money is a life-belt thrown to a swimmer who has already reached the shore in safety".

Medicine

George Bernard Shaw's belief was that: "We have not lost faith, but we have transferred it from God to the medical profession".

Positioning

The economist Thomas Michael Kettle [1880–1916] wrote: "My only counsel to Ireland is that, to become deeply Irish, it must become European".

Anticonsumerism

An Irish proverb says: "Enough and no waste is as good as a feast".

Inflation

In *Essay on the Nature of Trade in General* published in 1755, Richard Cantillon explained that: "In consequence it would appear that when a state grows by trade and the abundance of money increases excessively the price of land and labor, the prince or the legislator should put aside money, keep it for unforeseen contingencies, and use all means to delay its circulation".[2]

Confidentiality

An Irish proverb warns that: *Is fearr cogar i gcluais Nora ná liú ón gcnoc is aired* ("A whisper in Nora's ear is as good as a shout from the highest hill"), meaning that as soon as you tell someone a secret, it is no longer a secret.

Mistakes

According to Jonathan Swift: "You should never be ashamed to admit you have been wrong. It only proves you are wiser today than yesterday".

Samuel Beckett had this to say: "Ever tried. Ever failed. No matter. Try Again. Fail again. Fail better".

[2]Cantillon, Richard (1755), *Essai sur la nature du commerce en général*, translated, edited and with an introduction by Antoin E. Murphy, and published in 2015 by the Libery Fund under the title *Essay on the Nature of Trade in General*, https://oll.libertyfund.org/title/essay-on-the-nature-of-trade-in-general-lf-ed

Slovakia

Nationalism

The Lutheran pastor, politician, archaeologist, and philosopher Jan Kollar [1793–1852] believed that nationalism led to hatred, aggression, and war. He described nationalism in these terms: "The bitter and agonizing fruit from the tree of nationality…".

The politician and writer Ľudovít Štúr [1815–1856] considered that: "National vanity not possessing in itself a deeper foundation is empty. It is, after all, about humanity, of which we are members in the same way as all other nations".

Cycles

According to Ľudovít Štúr: "For nature, after every summer, there is autumn and finally winter; this sequence also appears in the history of the world. Nations, exhausted by the heat and work, gradually leave the stage of history, and there follows an interval, a spiritual winter when life comes to an end… However, the evolution of humanity continues, and eternal truths do not collapse, on the contrary: after the winter, just as the arrival of spring sees nature awaken to abundant life and begin with renewed strength, so it is with the life of humanity".

Endurance

According to Ľudovít Štúr: "Nothing great, nothing beautiful, nothing noble has been created without sacrifice; only the weak cannot learn to sacrifice themselves, not the noble soul that burns for this, for it is in sacrifice that the spirit shows its power, its domination".

C. Peicuti, *The European Economy in 100 Quotes*, Contributions to Economics,
https://doi.org/10.1007/978-3-031-68819-5_27

Governance

In 1846, Ľudovít Štúr wrote: "There is no happiness in towering above others and in oppressing others, for happiness is sharing life with others who are equally educated, equally happy, equally contented".

Budget

According to Slovakia's Prime Minister Ľudovít Ódor [1976–]: "A balanced budget is like a highway from Bratislava to Košice. Already, it will be, but in the end some tunnel will always make it more complicated".[1]

According to Lydia Šimková: "It is good to be in debt to the State when this debt won't be paid by the politicians, but by the country's citizens".[2]

Unemployment

Štefan Luby [1941–] considers that: "The invisible hand of the market can create jobs, but the invisible foot of the market can kick us out of them".[3]

Unemployment

Ján Fekete Apolkin takes a humorous look at the transition from a planned economy with food shortages, but guaranteed work, to a market economy with unemployment: "We got into the habit of queuing for bananas. No cause for regrets. At least, that got us trained for queuing outside job centres".[4]

Author Zdena Kalčíková ironizes about the inefficiency of the employment agency: "The job centre will definitely find us a job: running around the offices".[5]

---

[1] https://www.odor.sk/svk/ekonomia/178/medialny-trojboj

[2] Šimková, Lydia (2023), from Literárny Týždenník (Journal of the Association of Slovak Writers), ref. LT 11–12 z 28. 4. 2023, source: https://www.literarny-tyzdennik.sk/zanre/aforizmy/

[3] Luby, Štefan, *Aphorims, Good Words, Maxims.*

[4] Apolkin, Ján Fekete (2018), from Literárny Týždenník (Journal of the Association of Slovak Writers), ref. LT 1–2 zo 17. 1. 2018, source: https://www.literarny-tyzdennik.sk/zanre/aforizmy/

[5] Kalčíková, Zdena (2018), from Literárny Týždenník (Journal of the Association of Slovak Writers), ref. LT 23–24 z 20. 6. 2018, source: https://www.literarny-tyzdennik.sk/zanre/aforizmy/

Money

Štefan Luby believes that: "Not having money to throw around is easy. It is more difficult to have money and spend usefully".[6]

According to the physicist: "Who takes quickly, takes twice".[7]

Peter Gossányi's view is that: "A thousand boomerangs are more likely to return to the thrower than a thousand euro to the lender".[8]

Tax

According to Štefan Luby: "Taxpayer is the current expression for the historical *misera contribuens plebs*".[9]

Poverty

From blogger Ľubica Rusnáková: "Slovakia has declared war on poverty. So far it is losing".[10]

Country

In December 2022, author Milan Kenda [1937–] asked: "What characterizes current Slovakia? High inflation and low self confidence".[11]

In 2021, Josef Bily wrote: "It seems the government has prepared a good plan for the reconstruction of our country for the European Union. However, it is doubtful it can put together a plan to restore trust with its citizens".[12]

[6] Luby, Štefan, *Aphorims, Proverbs, Maxims.*

[7] Ibid.

[8] Gossányi, Peter (2017), from Literárny Týždenník (Journal of the Association of Slovak Writers), ref. LT 27–28 z 23. 8. 2017, source: https://www.literarny-tyzdennik.sk/zanre/aforizmy/

[9] Luby, Štefan, *Aphorims, Good Words, Maxims.*

[10] Source: https://blog.sme.sk/lubicarusnakova/sukromne/aforizmy-vsednych-dni

[11] Kenda, Milan (2022), from Literárny Týždenník (Journal of the Association of Slovak Writers), ref. LT 39–40 z 8. 12. 2022, source: https://www.literarny-tyzdennik.sk/zanre/aforizmy/

[12] Bily, Josef (2022), from Literárny Týždenník (Journal of the Association of Slovak Writers), ref. LT 33–34 zo 26. 10. 2022, source: https://www.literarny-tyzdennik.sk/zanre/aforizmy/

He has also asked: "Is foreign capital for funeral services? Yes, when burying Slovak national pride".[13]

Spending

In 2022, author Ján Marsálek declared: "Culture comes first... when it's about cutting costs".[14]

Micro and Macro

In the article *What the coronas have taught us*, Zuzana Brnoliaková writes: "Even a microscopic enemy can have macroeconomic consequences".[15]

Inequalities

According to Author Milan Kupecky: "Liberal social policy: big size mesh for the social security net, small size mesh for the soup".[16]

According to Josef Bily: "What divides people is dissatisfaction over distribution".[17]

Wages

According to Peter Gossányi: "The best-paid are the actors performing in the political arena".[18]

[13] Bily, Josef (2019), from Literárny Týždenník (Journal of the Association of Slovak Writers), ref. LT 11–12 z 27. 3. 2019, source: https://www.literarny-tyzdennik.sk/zanre/aforizmy/

[14] Marsálek, Ján (2022), from Literárny Týždenník (Journal of the Association of Slovak Writers), ref. LT 7–8 zo 2. 3. 2022, source: https://www.literarny-tyzdennik.sk/zanre/aforizmy/

[15] Zuzana Brnoliaková (2020), from Literárny Týždenník (Journal of the Association of Slovak Writers), ref. LT 27–28 z 19. 8. 2020, source: https://www.literarny-tyzdennik.sk/zanre/aforizmy/

[16] Kupecky, Milan (2023), from Literárny Týždenník (Journal of the Association of Slovak Writers), ref. LT 5–6 z 22 1. 2023, source: https://www.literarny-tyzdennik.sk/zanre/aforizmy/

[17] Bily, Josef (2022), from Literárny Týždenník (Journal of the Association of Slovak Writers), ref. LT 5–6 z 15. 2. 2017, source: https://www.literarny-tyzdennik.sk/zanre/aforizmy/

[18] Gossányi, Peter (2016), from Literárny Týždenník (Journal of the Association of Slovak Writers), ref. LT 31–32 zo 28. 9. 2016, source: https://www.literarny-tyzdennik.sk/zanre/aforizmy/

Pavel Fábry has this to say: "A word of advice for your wallet: do you want to earn more than your salary or pension? Migrate!"[19]

Integrity

For Imrich Kupec: "The quality of society depends on people who have no market value: one category must not be able to be bought, and the other must not be for sale...".[20]

[19] Fábry, Pavel (2015), from Literárny Týždenník (Journal of the Association of Slovak Writers), ref. LT 33–34 zo 26. 10. 2022, source: https://www.literarny-tyzdennik.sk/zanre/aforizmy/

[20] Imrich Kupec (2015), from Literárny Týždenník (Journal of the Association of Slovak Writers), ref. LT 25–26 zo 1. 7. 2015, source: https://www.literarny-tyzdennik.sk/zanre/aforizmy/

Latvia

Economic System

Following the restoration of Latvia's independence in 1991, and as explained by Valdis Dombrovskis [1971–], who served as the country's Finance Minister from 2002 to 2004, then as its Prime Minister from 2009 to 2014, and who was appointed as the European Commissioner for Trade in 2019: "Establishing a functioning economy was vital for the newly reborn nation. Its reform package contained standard elements of systemic change: liberalization of prices and trade, macroeconomic stabilization, and privatization. All kinds of national institutions and legislation had to be established, often from scratch".[1]

The economist Raita Karnīte [1949–] explains: "The early 1990s were a time of hope, opportunity and collapse. When the great economic transformation began, few understood what it meant, what it would be and what it would bring. In the beginning, it was about freedom, reclaiming one's country and national sovereignty. The opening of borders, reunions with separated loved ones, general emotional uplift and hope of a better life - all these as gifts!"[2]

The historian and economist Arnolds Aizsilnieks [1898–1982] wrote: "When they set out to revitalise and build the Latvian national economy, those who determine Latvian economic policy did not consider it possible to be guided by the purely economic objective of increasing national income. They gave priority to national political objectives, in order to consolidate and secure the independence acquired by the Latvian people".[3]

---

[1] Åslund, Anders, and Dombrovskis, Validis (2011), *How Latvia Came through the Financial Crisis*, Peterson Institute for International Economics, 2011, p.7.

[2] Krūmiņš, Gatis (Editor) (2017), *Histoire de l'économie lettone*, Riga, p. 393.

[3] Aizsilnieks, Arnolds (1968), *Histoire économique de la Lettonie*, 1914–1945, Stockholm, p.960.

C. Peicuti, *The European Economy in 100 Quotes*, Contributions to Economics,
https://doi.org/10.1007/978-3-031-68819-5_28

Historians Gatis Krūmiņš [1973–] and Aivars Stranga [1954–] have another reading: "During this period (the 20th century), the different sectors of the Latvian economy, as well as society as a whole, demonstrated an astonishing ability to adapt and survive in widely contrasting circumstances, no matter how foolish the decisions taken by the political authorities".[4]

Cycles

The market economy is unstable and cyclical. Vaira Vīķe Freiberga [1937–], who was Latvia's President from 1999 to 2007, drew attention to the error of not putting aside resources at the cycle peak that would be available to cushion a cyclical downturn. Historian Gatis Krūmiņš recalled this episode: "It is to be hoped that Latvia's future prime ministers will have a better understanding of the Old Testament parable used by the then President of Latvia who tried in vain to convince the then Prime Minister that Pharaoh's dream of seven cows, sleek and fat, followed by seven cows, ugly and gaunt, could be just as prophetic in our time. At the time, the Prime Minister only latched onto the idea of the fat years, not heeding the advice to be fiscally responsible and to prepare for future challenges, even during the fat years. Live life, learn life!"[5]

Repositioning

Valdis Birkavs [1942–], who served as Prime Minister from 1993 to 1994, explains that: "The evolution of capitalism in today's over-populated world, along with decreasing resources and fewer territories, requires a new philosophy, new political and economic approaches and a new education system".[6]

In 2016, Juris Ozoliņš, who was Latvia's Energy Minister from 1994 to 1995, and then chaired the country's Energy Security Commission from 2016 to 2019, has this to say: "The integration process covers all sectors of the economy. Education and science must be at the forefront. At the same time, we must not repeat the mistakes of the last two decades by stubbornly trying to invent a special path for Latvia's development".

[4]Ijab, I., Kusber, J., Misan, I., and Oberlander, E. (2018), *Lettonie 1918–2018: un siècle d'existence*, Riga, p.277.

[5]Krūmiņš, Gatis (2017), *Histoire de l'économie lettone*, Riga, p.663–664.

[6]https://news.lv/The_Baltic_Times/2018/07/31/i-dont-exclude-possibility-each-three-baltic-countries-will-follow-their-own-path

Crises

Crises can be real opportunities if one knows how to take advantage of them. In this respect, the economist Mārtiņš Kazāks [1973–], who has served as the Governor of Latvijas Banka since December 2019, stated: "There have been crises and there will be more - the main thing is not to let them go to waste!"[7]

Precariat

Precariat is a neologism, a portmanteau term obtained by merging precarity with proletariat.

Philosopher and historian Ivars Šuvajevs [1963–] wrote: "Although it is perfectly legitimate to ask whether capitalism still exists today, it is now much more common to speak of the precariat than the proletariat".[8]

Consumerism

Ivars Šuvajevs observed: "The poor are as poor as the rich. Today, consumerism holds sway, characterised not by judicious choices but by spending for spending's sake, which creates a spendthrift individual who is just as burdened by poverty as by wealth".[9]

---

[7] Krūmiņš, Gatis (2017), *Histoire de l'économie lettone*, Riga, p.705.

[8] Shuvaevs, Ivars (2013), *La description de la présence: la quête des valeurs et de l'identité*, Riga, p.14.

[9] Shuvaev, Ivars (2013). *La description de la présence: la quête des valeurs et de l'identité*, Riga, 2013, p.137.

Portugal

Gold

Considered to be Portugal's greatest poet, Luis de Camões [1525–1580], who lived at a time when Portugal rivalled the great European kingdoms thanks to its armada, lamented:

> Gold conquers the strongest citadels,
> Turns friends into traitors and liars;
> Persuades the noblest to acts of infamy,
> Betraying their leaders to the enemy;
> It corrupts maidens, who ignore
> The threat to honour or reputation;
> Even scholarship at times has been bought,
> Blinding discernment and impartial thought.
> It glosses and glozes authorities
> Subtly making and unmaking laws;
> It leads people to perjure themselves
> And makes tyrants of a thousand kings;
> Even of those sworn only to God
> Countless more times you will hear
> How this enchanter can corrupt and tarnish
> But all the while preserving virtue's varnish![1]

The Jesuit priest António Vieira [1608–1697], the greatest Portuguese writer of the seventeenth century, had this to say: "Fortune is never a match for man's desire".

[1]Camões, Luís Vaz de (1997), *The Lusiads*, translated by Landeg White, Oxford: Oxford University Press.

C. Peicuti, *The European Economy in 100 Quotes*, Contributions to Economics,
https://doi.org/10.1007/978-3-031-68819-5_29

Wealth

In *Viagens na Minha Terra,*[2] the Portuguese poet and playwright Almeida Garrett [1799–1854] wrote: "I ask the political economists and the moralists if they have ever calculated the number of individuals who must be condemned to misery, overwork, demoralisation, degradation, rank ignorance, overwhelming misfortune and utter penury in order to produce one rich man".[3]

Education

António Vieira: "A good education is gold. Wherever you go, it has value".

Respect

António Vieira drew attention to the fact that: "The restoration of respect is much more difficult than the gifting of money".

Results

For António Vieira: "The fruit harvested is in the image of the work accomplished".

Change

In the poem *Mudam-se os Tempos, Mudam-se as Vontades,*[4] Luis de Camões explained that the only constraint in man's life was change:

> Times change, as do our wills,
> What we are is ever-changing;
> All the world is made of change,
> And forever attaining new qualities.
> We continuously see new things,
> Different in everything from hope;
> Of the bad are the sorrows in remembrance,
> And the good, if any, nostalgia.

---

[2] *Travels to My Homeland.*

[3] Garrett, Almeida (2012), *Viagens na Minha Terra,* Martin Claret.

[4] *Times Change, Wills Change.*

And he goes on:

Time covers the ground with a green mantle,
That was once covered with cold snow,
And finally, it converts the sweet song into tears.
And, apart from this changing each day,
Another change makes me astonished:
That life does not change as it used to.

Reputation

In the epic poem *Os Lusíadas*[5] published in 1572, which reflects on Vasco de Gama's discovery of the sea route to the Indies and other episodes in Portugal's history, in the tradition of Homer's *Iliad* and *Odyssey*, later Virgil's *Aeneid*, Luis de Camões wrote:

O pride of power! O futile lust
For that vanity known as fame!
That hollow conceit which puffs itself up
And which popular cant calls honour!
What punishment, what poetic justice,
You exact on souls that pursue you!
To what death, what miseries you condemn
Your heroes! What pains you inflict on them!
You wreck all peace of soul and body,
You promote separation and adultery;
Subtly, manifestly, you consume
The wealth of kingdoms and empires!
They call distinction, they call honour
What deserves ridicule and contempt;
They talk of glory and eternal fame,
And men are driven frantic by a name![6]

And going on:

For indeed, it is through such perils,
Such wearisome and fearful labours,
That those for whom fame is the spur
Achieve honours and lasting esteem;
Not be depending on an ancient name
Or a long lineage of ancestors,
Nor sprawling on gold beds made comfortable
By furs of the finest Russian sable [...][7]

---

[5] *The Lusiads.*

[6] Camões, Luís Vaz de (1997), *The Lusiads*, translated by Landeg White, Oxford: Oxford University Press.

[7] Ibid.

Jesuit priest António Vieira, who took a stand against the all-powerful Inquisition in his time and was a relentless critic of slavery, pointed out that it is not honorific portrait statues erected by the authorities that make a reputation, but the appreciation of one's peers: "Cato had no statue on the Capitol. Foreigners came to Rome, saw the statues of famous men, but asked about Cato. These questions were the biggest statue of all. The Senate erected a statue for the others, the world erected a statue for Cato".

Pride

In the *Os Mistérios de Lisboa*[8] published in 1854, Portuguese writer Camilo Castelo Branco [1825–1890] explained that: "Pride, in a poor man, is a terrible passion. In the rich man, it spreads in splendour that dazzles his enemies. In the poor, it aspires to a gnawing vengeance, when it does not slowly consume him".

Curiosity

Curiosity is inseparable from the entrepreneurial spirit. As Portuguese writer José Maria de Eça de Queiroz [1845–1900] explained: "Curiosity leads to everything: sometimes to eavesdropping, sometimes to discovering America".

Endeavour

Words of advice from Fernando Pessoa [1888–1935]: "Be whole in everything. Put all you are into the smallest thing you do".

António Vieira wrote: "If you serve your country, which has been ungrateful to you, you have done what you had to, it has done what it must".

Prophesy

In *História do Futuro*,[9] António Vieira wrote: "The world will hear what it has never seen, read what it has never heard, admire what it has never read, and marvel at what it has never imagined".

[8] *Mysteries of Lisbon.*

[9] *Preliminary Book to the History of the Future.*

Communication

António Vieira drew attention to the supremacy of images over words: "What enters through the ears is created, what enters through the eyes is made manifest".

He therefore advises priests to deliver sermons laden with imagery: "Don't you know, priests, why our sermons do not touch the people's hearts? Because we do not preach to the eyes, only to the ears".

In the final analysis, however, actions speak louder than words, for as António Vieira pointed out: "Words are enough to speak to the wind; deeds are necessary to speak to the heart".

Generosity

Generosity is the key to the success of any undertaking. As stressed by António Vieira: "Generous deeds, not illustrious parents, are the hallmarks of gentlemen".

Time

In *O Homem Duplicado*,[10] José de Sousa Saramago [1922–2010], the recipient of the 1998 Nobel Prize in Literature, commented: "People often say, Let time do its work, but what we always forget to ask is if there will ever be enough time".[11]

Chance

For José de Sousa Saramago: "Chance doesn't choose, it proposes".[12]

Strategy

To embark on an undertaking means creating, and daring to pursue your dreams and ideas to the end. The advice from José de Sousa Saramago: "Let yourself be guided by the child you were. The child is something that is someone who is no more".[13]

---

[10] *The Double.*

[11] Saramago, José (2004), *The Double*, Harcourt.

[12] Saramago, José (1999), *All the Names*, Harcourt.

[13] Saramago, José (2015), *Small Memories*, Harvill Secker.

Experience

Luis de Camões explained that: "The art of war is not learned from books, or in the silence of a monastic retreat". He added: "War is studied on the battlefields".

According to José de Sousa Saramago: "You don't know the fruit by the rind, but by sinking your teeth into it".

International Commerce

Arthur Dunkel [1932–2005] served as director-general of the General Agreement on Tariffs and Trade (GATT) between 1980 and 1993. GATT is a legal agreement signed in 1947, which remained in force until 1994. It was replaced by the World Trade Organization from 1995 onwards.

For Arthur Dunkel: "Regionalism and multilateralism are two sides of the same coin".[14]

GATT was intended to prevent a return to protectionism (which was responsible for worsening the crisis of the 1930s), by lowering barriers to trade, particularly customs duties. Over time, the number of GATT signatory countries increased from 23 to 128, reducing the average level of tariffs on the manufactured goods of industrialised countries from 40% to less than 5%.

As explained by Arthur Dunkel in 1989: "Endless negotiations on lowering a customs duty by two or three points, that was the GATT of old. Today, the stakes are global. All the economic agents are now concerned, starting with small and medium-sized businesses, the ones out of the running before they even get going in a world without rules or discipline. The aim is to give every producer the opportunity to sell on as large a market as possible, in the knowledge that if they have what it takes to win, they will actually be able to win. It is also to ensure that the buyers, now able to find out about everything that is being produced in the world, will be able to source themselves on the best possible terms".

---

[14] Dunkel, Arthur (1992), *Regionalism and multilateralism are two sides of the same coin - GATT surveillance ensures the coinage is not debased*, GATT Newsletter, September 1992, https://docs.wto.org/gattdocs/q/GG/GATTFOCUS/93.pdf

Norway

Econometrics

In the 1920s, Ragnar Frisch [1895–1973], who went on to share the 1969 Sveriges Riksbank Prize in Economic Sciences in Memory of Alfred Nobel with Jan Tinbergen "for having developed and applied dynamic models for the analysis of economic processes",[1] revived the project abandoned in 1912 and was one of the founders of the Econometric Society, an international network of mathematical economists. He defined econometrics as: "Intermediate between mathematics, statistics, and economics, we find a new discipline which, for lack of a better name, may be called econometrics. Econometrics has as its aim to subject abstract laws of theoretical political economy or 'pure' economics to experimental and numerical verification, and thus to turn pure economics, as far as possible, into a science in the strict sense of the word".

Concerned about how econometrics was being used, the Norwegian economist warned against what he termed "playometrics," writing: "I have insisted that econometrics must have relevance to concrete realities, otherwise it degenerates into something which is not worthy of the name econometrics, but ought rather to be called playometrics".

[1] Ragnar Frisch—Facts. NobelPrize.org. Nobel Prize Outreach AB 2023. https://www.nobelprize.org/prizes/economic-sciences/1969/frisch/facts/

C. Peicuti, *The European Economy in 100 Quotes*, Contributions to Economics,
https://doi.org/10.1007/978-3-031-68819-5_30

Macroeconomics and Microeconomics

Composed of three Greek words—*makros* meaning 'long, abnormally large, on a large scale', *oikos* which is usually translated as 'household', and *nemein*, which is best translated as 'management and dispensation'—the term 'macroeconomics' was coined by Ragnar Frisch by opposition to 'microeconomics', another term coined by the Norwegian economist—derived from the Greek *micros* meaning 'small in size'.

Most importantly, Ragnar Frisch was adamant that macroeconomics must not be studied as an aggregation of all microeconomics, i.e., the economics of aggregates: "Indeed, it is always possible by a suitable system of subscripts and superscripts, etc., to introduce practically all factors which we may imagine: all individual commodities, all individual entrepreneurs, all individual consumers, etc., and to write out various kinds of relationships between these magnitudes, taking care that the number of equations is equal to the number of variables. Such a theory, however, would only have a rather limited interest. In such a theory it would hardly be possible to study such fundamental problems as the exact time shape of the solutions, the question of whether one group of phenomena is lagging behind or leading before another group, the question of whether one part of the system will oscillate with higher amplitudes than another part, and so on. [...] In order to attack these problems on a macro-dynamic basis so as to explain the movement of the system taken in its entirety, we must deliberately disregard a considerable amount of the details of the picture. We may perhaps start by throwing all kinds of production into one variable, all consumption into another, and so on, imagining that the notions 'production', 'consumption', and so on, can be measured by some sort of total indices".[2]

Cycles

His analyses of business cycles and impulse propagation via investment became one of the principles of Real Business Cycle theories: "The majority of the economic oscillations which we encounter seem to be explained most plausibly as free oscillations. In many cases, they seem to be produced by the fact that certain exterior impulses hit the economic mechanism and thereby initiate more or less regular oscillations.

The most important feature of the free oscillations is that the length of the cycles and the tendency towards dampening are determined by the intrinsic structure of the swinging system, while the intensity (the amplitude) of the fluctuations is determined primarily by the exterior impulse. An important consequence of this is that a

---

[2]Frisch, Ragnar (1933), *Propagation Problems and Impulse Problems in Dynamic Economics*, in Economic Essays in Honor of Gustav Cassel.

more or less regular fluctuation may be produced by a cause which operates irregularly. There need not be any synchronism between the initiating force or forces and the movement of the swinging system. This fact has frequently been overlooked in economic cycle analysis".[3]

He goes on: "If a cyclical variation is analysed from the point of view of a free oscillation, we have to distinguish between two fundamental problems: first, the propagation problem; second, the impulse problem. The propagation problem is the problem of explaining by the structural properties of the swinging system what the character of the swings would be in case the system was started in some initial situation. This must be done by an essentially dynamic theory, that is to say, by a theory that explains how one situation grows out of the foregoing".[4]

In *Propagation Problems and Impulse Problems in Dynamic Economics* published in 1933, Ragnar Frisch explained that: "If you hit a rocking horse with a stick, the movement of the horse will be very different from that of the stick".

Norwegian economist Finn E. Kydland [1943–] shared the 2004 Sveriges Riksbank Prize in Economic Sciences in Memory of Alfred Nobel with American economist Edward Prescott [1940–2022] "for their contributions to dynamic macroeconomics: the time consistency of economic policy and the driving forces behind business cycles".[5]

In 1990, Kydland declared that: "One thing we have learned is that business cycles are not that costly to people. The welfare implications are not that big—at least from normal business cycles. That's not to say, of course, that governments can't implement bad policies and make things much worse. But it may behoove us to devote more attention to longer-run questions where the benefits can be really great. As our understanding of economic theory improves and as computers improve, it is natural to turn our attention to things that matter over the life cycle, such as social security, immigration, age and wealth distribution, and so on".[6]

[3]Ibid.

[4]Ibid.

[5]The Sveriges Riksbank Prize in Economic Sciences in Memory of Alfred Nobel 2004. NobelPrize.org. Nobel Prize Outreach AB 2023. https://www.nobelprize.org/prizes/economic-sciences/2004/summary/

[6]https://www.elibrary.imf.org/view/journals/023/0034/009/article-A010-en.xml

Appendix

Cristina

C. Peicuti, *The European Economy in 100 Quotes*, Contributions to Economics,
https://doi.org/10.1007/978-3-031-68819-5

Roberta, Irene, Sabrina, Maelle, Cristina, Marko, Guy and Stefanie

Lina, Marta, Celeste, Graham, Roberta, David, Sabrina, Michal, Edna, Cristina, Desiree, Marko, Milena, Irene, Natasa, Maelle, Jennifer

Cristina, Stefanie, Maelle and Celeste

Mariya, Edna, Ray, Ewelina, Milena

Ewelina, Milena, Cristina, Roberta and Maelle

Cristina, Maelle, Jennifer, Guy, Marko, Sabrina, Roberta and Irene

Eleni, Eleni, Marko, Cristina, Milena, Lina, Edna, Elias, Miguel, Natasa, Nicolas, Stefanie, Jennifer, Ewelina, Roberta, Desire, Alex, Irene

Jennifer, Roberta, Guy, Cristina and Stefanie

Jennifer and Roberta

Ewelina, Edna, Cristina, Milena and Irena

Sabrina, Cristina, Marko, Guy and Stefanie (Roberta behind)

Guy, Roberta, Ray

Back: Maelle, Roberta, Stefanie, Ray, Cristina; Front: Jennifer, Guy, Marko

Marta, Mariya, Roberta, Celeste, Natasa, Ray, Sonja

Guy, Marko, Ray

Maelle, Irene, Cristina, Jennifer, Stefanie, Roberta

Roberta and Cristina

Bibliography

Goethe, Johann Wolfgang von, *Faust*, translated by Gérard de Nerval, complete version volumes 1 et 2, Kindle edition.
Orieux, Jean (1998), *Talleyrand, ou, Le sphinx incompris*, Flammarion.
Tosi, Renzo (2010), *Dictionnaire des sentences latines et grecques*, Jérôme Million.
Verne, Jules (2002), *Paris au XXe siècle*, Le livre de Poche.
Weber, Max (2013), *L'éthique protestante et l'esprit du capitalisme*, Format Kindle, Presses Électroniques de France.
Zola, Émile (1954), *L'Argent*, édition Fasquelle.

Webography

Prix Nobel website, https://www.nobelprize.org/

With our thanks to

Carol I Central University Library, https://www.bcub.ro/en/home/
Library of Catalonia, https://www.bnc.cat/
Mihai Eminescu Central University Library of Iași, https://www.bcu-iasi.ro/en/
National Library of Luxembourg, https://bnl.public.lu/fr.html
National and Universty Library in Zagreb, www.nsk.hr
National Library of the Czech Republic, https://www.en.nkp.cz/
National Library of Estonia, https://www.rara.ee/en/
National Library of Latvia, https://www.lnb.lv/
National Library of Lithuania, https://www.lnb.lt/en/
National Széchényi Library, https://www.oszk.hu/en
Slovak National Library, https://www.snk.sk/en/
National and University Library Slovenia, www.nuk.uni-lj.si
Royal Danish Library, https://www.kb.dk/en

C. Peicuti, *The European Economy in 100 Quotes*, Contributions to Economics,
https://doi.org/10.1007/978-3-031-68819-5

Index

C. Peicuti, *The European Economy in 100 Quotes*, Contributions to Economics,
https://doi.org/10.1007/978-3-031-68819-5

The manufacturer's authorised representative in the EU is Springer Nature Customer Service Centre GmbH, Europaplatz 3, 69115 Heidelberg, Germany. If you have any concerns regarding our products, please contact ProductSafety@springernature.com

Printed and bound by CPI Group (UK) Ltd, Croydon, CR0 4YY
01/10/2026
02225913-0010